# Getting My Heart Right With God

## Bill Bagents

CYPRESS

Copyright © 2023 by Bill Bagents

Manufactured in the United States of America

Cataloging-in-Publication Data

Bagents, Bill (William Ronald), 1956–

Getting my heart right with God / Bill Bagents

p. cm.

ISBN 978-1-956811-45-2 (pbk.) 978-1-956811-46-9 (ebook)

1. God (Christianity). 2. Christian life. I. Author. II. Title.

248.4—dc20

Library of Congress Control Number: 2023937511

Cover design by Brad McKinnon and Brittany Vander Maas.

Cypress Publications
PO Box HCU
3625 Helton Drive
Florence, AL 35630

www.hcu.edu/publications

*This book is dedicated to all the kind people who help me write, especially Laura Bagents, Brad McKinnon, and the students at Heritage Christian University.*

# Contents

# Introduction

The essays in this book were written over some twenty years. Most were first published as chapters in books, articles in periodicals, or lessons for Bible classes. With one exception, "God as Counselor," they don't come from books where I was the primary author.

At least four of the essays have not yet been published elsewhere. Several of the others have been notably revised. For the lessons that originally included discussion questions, those were left intact. For the sake of uniformity and to invite a fresh reading of the text, all Bible quotations have been converted to the English Standard Version. As you likely know, the wisest students read from multiple translations. It's an excellent deterrent to idiosyncratic misreading, and it often sparks enhanced understanding.

The four-part division of the book—God, Grace, Service, and Leadership—is somewhat arbitrary. God is both the fountain and the foundation of grace, service, and leadership. Without Him, nothing else matters. That helps explain why the sections are uneven, with essays on God predominating.

How might this book be used?

In terms of settings, please think of individual study, family Bible study, and Bible class. In terms of practice, check behind the author (Acts 17:11). Are the passages cited appropriate and rightly handled (2 Tim 2:15)? Are any twisted or otherwise misapplied (2 Pet 3:16)? What texts should have been cited to strengthen the point at hand?

In terms of purpose, please think of spiritual formation —part of drawing near to God and inviting Him to draw near to us. Think also of enhanced knowledge of Scripture. As you explore and add your experience and wisdom to the essays, you'll read a better book than I have written.

Please don't limit yourself by seeking knowledge for the sake of knowledge. We learn so we can better serve our Lord. Our aim is always to practice what God commands and to teach what He reveals. In God's goodness, using what we learn to bless others always takes us to the next level of understanding.

# God

# Chapter 1

## *God the Master Servant*

From the beginning, the Almighty has demonstrated a servant's heart. Not only did he notice that it was not good that man be alone, but He also acted to provide a stunningly appropriate companion (Gen 2:18). Even as Adam and Eve were banned from the Garden for their sin, God provided adequate clothing for them (Gen 3:21). When Eve bore Cain, she realized that she had—again—been cared for by God (Gen 4:1). When Cain expressed despair over banishment for his sin and fear of death, God gave him a mark of protection (Gen 4:13–15). What an image! The righteous judge chooses to bless the guilty man who has stained His creation with innocent blood.

Biblical examples of God's loving service to his creatures abound. We think of God's protection of Abraham and Sarah (Gen 12–22). He preserved life during nomadic travels in a hostile land, He multiplied their possessions, and He reaffirmed His gracious promises during a 25-year wait. He even pulled back the curtain to show some future events to Abraham (Gen 18:16–21).

God had no need to show Jacob the dream of the ladder ascending to heaven (Gen 28). Jacob, on the other hand, had the stunning need to meet the God who was protecting and directing him. God's protection of Jacob included the dream of warning given to Laban (31:24, 29). The Lord's protection of/care for Jacob peaked in the famous wrestling episode of Genesis 32:22–32, where Jacob's ability to defend himself was greatly diminished (his damaged hip), but his confidence in God's protection was greatly enhanced. God repeatedly reached out to Jacob with financial, physical, emotional, and spiritual support.

The Joseph saga is a rich story of promise and providence, of faith and forgiveness. God put Joseph where he needed to be to preserve the lives of His chosen people (Gen 5:19–20). God accomplished for Joseph and his family what they had neither the means nor the foresight to accomplish for themselves.

Bible believers value God's stellar service to Israel during the Exodus. When they had no army, He used the Red Sea to crush their enemies. He led them from Egypt to Canaan on a route of His choice that protected them from early and potentially devastating hostilities (Exod 13:17–18). The Lord served them manna six days a week. Their protein came through the quail He sent. God served them by providing and empowering leaders from Moses and Aaron to Joshua and Caleb. And those blessings continued through the period of the conquest. We particularly note God's encouragement of Joshua in Joshua 1:1–9 and 7:6–15.

Bible believers recognize the cycle of sin-punishment-repentance-deliverance in the book of Judges. Time and again, God gave His people both the deliverer and the deliverance that they needed. He showed amazing grace and the highest level of longsuffering. The story of Gideon stands as a remarkable example of God's patient service while calling a reluctant leader. Though a clear miracle of fire had already established the identity of God's angel (Judg 6:19–24), God still permitted Gideon to request two additional signs (Judg 6:30–40). While we do not recommend testing God in this manner, we take heart in God's willingness to meet Gideon's needs and to help His servant overcome his doubts.

# 1 Kings 19: A Powerful Test Case

Few Old Testament examples of God reaching down from Heaven to serve one of His servants can rival 1 Kings 19. Elijah fled in despair when Jezebel ordered his death. He believed that he was alone and that hope was gone (1 Kgs 19:10). In what ways did God serve Elijah?

An angel's touch awakened Elijah. God provided a baked cake and a jar of water (1 Kgs 19:6). After Elijah rested again, there was a second meal accompanied by encouraging words (1 Kgs 19:7–8). God enabled that meal to sustain the prophet for forty days (1 Kgs 19:8). God provided three powerful demonstrations of His power (1 Kgs 19:11–12). He recommissioned Elijah, giving him multiple important assignments (1 Kgs 19:15–16). He promised judgment and justice (1 Kgs 19:17). God corrected Elijah's errant thinking, reminding him of 7,000 additional faithful men (1 Kgs 19:18). And he gave Elijah a co-worker (1 Kgs 19:19). It would be difficult to imagine a more well-rounded and effective set of encouraging actions!

## Surprising Service

Examples of God's service are not limited to the faithful. 2 Kings 5 recounts God's healing of Naaman the leper. We remember that this is Naaman, the Syrian general to whom God had granted victory over Israel. Naaman's story is filled with surprising service. The Israeli captive who served Naaman's wife blessed her captor with word of a healing prophet in Israel. Naaman's servants blessed Naaman with bold, wise, and respectful counsel that helped him overcome his ego and seize God's mercy. The miraculous healing stands amazing, but so does God's powerful providential influence. The entire account emphasizes God's over-arching goodness and documents God's amazing grace in allowing humans to serve major roles in His unfolding plan.

Genesis 21:1–21 documents God's gracious service toward Hagar and Ishmael as they had been sent away from Abraham's camp. Their water was gone, and Hagar wept in anticipatory grief over the coming death of her son. Unless God had spoken a word of encouragement and opened her eyes to a nearby well, both would have perished.

Meeting Jonah's need for shade clearly was not God's primary goal in causing the plant to grow at his camp outside Nineveh (Jonah 4:7–11). The plant served as both object lesson and visual aid for the teaching that followed. God's challenge of Jonah's attitude leads our minds to Galatians 6:1–2 and the outstanding service of spiritual rescue.

These stories bring to mind the teaching of Jesus from Matthew 5:45: "For he makes his sun rise on the evil and on the good and sends rain on the just and on the unjust." Acts 17:28 applies equally: "In him we live and move and have our being." It is His earth on which we stand and His air that we breathe.

## Jesus–The Embodiment of God's Service

We love the challenging words of Matthew 20:25–28.

> But Jesus called them to him and said, "You know that the rulers of the Gentiles lord it over them, and their great ones exercise authority over them. It shall not be so among you. But whoever would be great among you must be your servant, and whoever would be first among you must be your slave, even as the Son of Man came not to be served but to serve, and to give his life as a ransom for

many.

We love the fact that the God who took on flesh and lived among us always honored those words (John 1:1–18, Phil 2:5–11).

Even before the time had come to begin His public ministry, Jesus rescued a wedding reception at the request of His mother (John 2:1–11). It requires little imagination to realize the embarrassment He prevented. John ensures that we do not miss the more important faith-building aspect of this sign (John 2:11).

Jesus's compassionate service to the multitudes is well documented in the gospels. Matthew 9:35–38 offers compassion as the reason for Jesus's healing and teaching. Matthew 14:13–21 offers compassion as the reason Jesus healed the sick and fed the 5,000. Matthew 15:29–39 documents the compassion of Jesus in healing and feeding 4,000 men in addition to women and children.

Each of these examples of divine love and service reflects Psalm 103:13, "As a father shows compassion to his children, so the Lord shows compassion to those who fear him." Jesus embodied the heart and service of His Father (Ps 135:13–14, Isa 63:7).

Matthew 4:23–24 summarizes Jesus's early service to those who were blessed by His presence:

And he went throughout all Galilee, teaching in their synagogues and proclaiming the gospel of the kingdom and healing every disease and every affliction among the people. So his fame spread throughout all Syria, and they brought him all the sick, those afflicted with various diseases and pains, those oppressed by demons, those having seizures, and paralytics, and he healed them.

Similarly, Luke 7:18–23 reads,

The disciples of John reported all these things to him. And John, calling two of his disciples to him, sent them to the Lord, saying, "Are you the one who is to come, or shall we look for another?" And when the men had come to him, they said, "John the Baptist has sent us to you, saying, 'Are you the one who is to come, or shall we look for another?'" In that hour he healed many people of diseases and plagues and evil spirits, and on many who were blind he bestowed sight. And he answered them, "Go and tell John what you have seen and heard: the blind receive their sight, the lame walk, lepers are cleansed, and the deaf hear, the dead are raised up, the poor have good news preached to them. And blessed is the one who is not offended by me."

Jesus knew that John would recognize the fulfillment of Isaiah 61:1–2, the very prophesies that Jesus read in the synagogue in Nazareth (Luke 4:16–21). No wonder Peter said of Jesus, "He went about doing good and healing all who were oppressed by the devil, for God was with him" (Acts 10:38)!

With no disrespect to any action of the Lord, we find

the service rendered to the exhausted and depleted woman of Mark 5:25–34 and to the widow of Nain particularly moving (Luke 7:11–17). The same can be said of Jesus's decision to touch the leper whom He healed (Mark 1:40–42). Even from the cross under maximum duress, He reached out to meet the needs of His mother (John 19:25–27). Reading beyond verse 27, the text seems to imply that Jesus's work was not finished until He arranged care for Mary—what love!

In perfect congruence with His actions, the teachings of Jesus promoted and honored service. In the judgment scene of Matthew 25, the differentiation between sheep and goats is described in terms of service.

> Then the righteous will answer him, saying, 'Lord, when did we see you hungry and feed you, or thirsty and give you drink? And when did we see you a stranger and welcome you, or naked and clothe you? And when did we see you sick or in prison and visit you?' And the King will answer them, "Truly, I say to you, as you did it to one of the least of these my brothers, you did it to me."

The Good Samaritan who loved his neighbor as himself is exemplary because of his compassionate and sacrificial service (Luke 10:25–37). The Good Samaritan sacrificed and put himself at both risk and inconvenience to serve a stranger. Even more importantly, the Good Shepherd sacrificed the prerogatives of divinity (Phil 2:5–11), took on the sins of the world (Isa 53, John 1:29), and gave His life blood for us—while we were His rebellious enemies (Rom 5:6–8). There can be no higher service nor any greater love (John 15:13)!

## A Stunning Pre-Cross Act of Service

As Jesus prepared His disciples for His death, He taught what may be the world's most surprising and stellar lessons on service. Through John, the Holy Spirit crafts the story beautifully.

> Now before the Feast of the Passover, when Jesus knew that his hour had come to depart out of this world to the Father, having loved his own who were in the world, he loved them to the end (John 13:1).

In full love and self-awareness, knowing that the cross, the denial, and the mass desertion were near, Jesus washed His disciples' feet.

This was neither grandstanding nor manipulation. Physically and culturally, it met the need of the moment. Spiritually, it did much more. It redefined greatness, value, worth, and success in terms of the kingdom of God. It put pride and posturing in their place. It stands as one of the ultimate examples of love over ego. It rejects "rights" in favor of humility.

How wise of Jesus to realize and state that the disciples did not grasp the meaning of His actions in this moment (John 13:12)! Though He made valiant effort to explain (John 13:13–17), many—to this very day—still do not understand. Jesus was not instituting a religious ritual. He was documenting that to follow God is to serve in any and every way that God allows.

## God's Ongoing Service

In what ways is God's service to His children ongoing? Three outstanding examples come to mind: prayer, providence, and preparation.

It is amazing to think of God as "on call" 24 x 7 x 365 worldwide from Day One until Jesus returns. He always hears our prayers. In that sense, the faithful are never alone, never forsaken, and never without help. Hebrews 13:5–6 quotes beautifully from Deuteronomy 31 and Psalm 118.

> Keep your life free from love of money, and be content with what you have, for he has said, "I will never leave you nor forsake you." So we can confidently say, "The Lord is my helper; I will not fear; what can man do to me?"

Not only does God always hear the faithful and the seeking, but He also hears even better than we pray.

> Likewise the Spirit helps us in our weakness. For we do not know what to pray for as we ought, but the Spirit himself intercedes for us with groanings too deep for

words. And he who searches hearts knows what is the mind of the Spirit, because the Spirit intercedes for the saints according to the will of God (Rom 8:26–27).

As if that were not sufficiently amazing, Jesus Christ also makes intercession for us from His place at God's right hand (Rom 8:34)! Could we imagine a loving service more precious or more powerful?

And to think that God not only hears our prayers, He often answers in ways that are wiser than our comprehension. And He uses even our prayers to shape our souls, to form us into the likeness of Christ.

God's providential service to His people is legendary —not in the sense of fictional, but in the sense of wondrous, amazing, and awe-inspiring. Through providence, God got Joseph to Egypt and saved countless lives (Gen 50:20). Through providence, God put Esther in place "for such a time as this" to save His people (Esth 4:14). Through providence, Ruth cared for Naomi, Naomi cared for Ruth, Boaz cared for both, and the joy of life was restored. Through providence, God moved Paul out of a deathtrap in Jerusalem and arranged free transportation to Rome—the city where he longed to preach the gospel (Acts 22–28).

Romans 8:28 strongly indicates God's ongoing providential care for His own. Though they are not authoritative and cannot carry the weight of Scripture, our experiences include blessings—care, service, and protection—from God that can be explained in no other way (Jas 1:17, Prov 3:5–6).

And what of God's service of preparation? As Christians, we treasure Jesus's words from John 14:1–4.

> Let not your hearts be troubled. Believe in God; believe also in me. In my Father's house are many rooms. If it were not so, would I have told you that I go to prepare a place for you? And if I go and prepare a place for you, I will come again and will take you to myself, that where I am you may be also. And you know the way to where I am going.

Please pardon the simple and obvious reasoning. The Godhead was able to create the universe in six days. Jesus Christ has had more than 2,000 years to work on the home He will give us in heaven. We find this amazingly encouraging!

Even with the magnificent descriptions of heaven within Revelation (Rev 21–22), we realize something of the challenge of describing spiritual reality in terms that humans can grasp. We view being with God the Father, God the Son, and God the Holy Spirit in a reality of endless perfection and delight as beyond all comprehension. Whatever we dream or imagine, heaven will be better. And the Lord is preparing such a place for us.

An Obvious, Practical Conclusion

From the beginning, God has served and blessed immeasurably. The Creator has taken care of His creatures at levels that we will never grasp. And He offers us the opportunity to reciprocate.

As surely as "we love because He first loved us" (1 John 4:10 and 19), we serve because He first served us. Scripture teaches this truth repeatedly.

> For we are his workmanship, created in Christ Jesus for good works, which God prepared beforehand, that we should walk in them (Eph 2:10).

John 9:4 with Matthew 10:25:

> We must work the works of him who sent me while it is day; night is coming, when no one can work. It is enough for the disciple to be like his teacher, and the servant like his master.

We get to be like Jesus. We get to love and serve like Jesus—and to His glory.

> "Beloved, I urge you as sojourners and exiles to abstain from the passions of the flesh, which wage war against your soul. Keep your conduct among the Gentiles honorable, so that when they speak against you as evildoers,

they may see your good deeds and glorify God on the day of visitation" (1 Pet 2:11–12).

"For the grace of God has appeared, bringing salvation for all people, training us to renounce ungodliness and worldly passions, and to live self-controlled, upright, and godly lives in the present age, waiting for our blessed hope, the appearing of the glory of our great God and Savior Jesus Christ, who gave himself for us to redeem us from all lawlessness and to purify for himself a people for his own possession who are zealous for good works" (Titus 2:11–14).

God, who first loved and served, calls and empowers us to love and serve. He accepts our service as sacrifices of praise to His name (Heb 13:3, 16). He wills that we continually love and serve as we await the return of His Son. And then He utterly and eternally loves and saves us in His land of perfect rest. Absolutely amazing!

## Note

This chapter first appeared as "God the Master Servant." Pages 40–52 in *Serving the Lord: A Festschrift for Freddie Patrick Moon and Janet Stewart Moon.* Heritage Legacy Series. Editors of Heritage Christian University Press. Florence, AL: Heritage Christian University Press, 2022.

# Chapter 2

## *God as Counselor*

One of the greatest examples of God's perfection is His humility in the midst of eternal perfection. The Almighty, who needs nothing and owes no one anything, chooses to interact with people—His rebellious and flawed creatures. We will examine some of God's interactions with people where His obvious intention was to help them. That's what we mean by "God as Counselor": God willingly and lovingly in the role of people helper, God both leading and serving by offering His help to those in both need and danger.

As we note these examples of God's actions, we'll address key questions. What is God modeling for us? What should we be learning from Him? Why is God doing what He's doing? How were His efforts received? What should we learn from how His efforts were received?

# God with Adam and Eve

Post sin, their eyes are opened, and the first people attempt to hide from God. It would be funny if it weren't so sad— trying to hide from the all-knowing omnipresent One. It isn't a case of the sinners seeking God for forgiveness. Rather, Genesis 3:9ff tells us that God comes seeking Adam and Eve. We know this because God asks, "Where are you?" (Gen 3:15)

"Where are you?" is the first of at least four questions that God poses for Adam and Eve. Often, we ask questions because we need information. It's never so with God. God, who is all-knowing, knows exactly where they are, exactly what they have done, the reasoning they employed (or failed to employ), and the motives from which they are acting. Why does God pose a series of questions? He asks to start a conversation, to give Adam and Eve opportunity to reflect, and to show them that He still loves them.

In His first people-helping conversation, God models the power of effective questions. Adam and Eve's responses leave much to be desired. Adam blames both Eve and God. Eve attempts to shift blame to the serpent and offers the excuse that she has been deceived. Still, we love the fact that God initiates the conversation and gives them the opportunity for truth, confession, and request for His help.

## God with Cain

Pre-murder, God sees the peril awaiting Cain. His feelings have been hurt, his sacrifice has been rejected, and he has looked bad before his family. Cain is angry. His face shows his pain (Gen 4:5). God knows that Cain's very soul is in danger.

Knowing the goodness of God, we're not surprised that He chooses to intervene. First, the Lord questions Cain's overall reaction, particularly his anger. "Why are you angry, and why has your face fallen?" (Gen 4:8) How should we hear those questions? Possibilities abound: "You would be wise to explore the nature of your anger. Are you angry with the right person—yourself?" "Are you angry in the right manner—angry that you have disappointed God?" "Are you angry in the right degree—angry enough to be motivated to repent, but not angry enough to compound your sin?"

Those who have tried to help angry people see the brilliance of God's questions. Anger often shuts down higher-order thinking. Inviting angry people to think invites them to step back from their anger. If people will think, they can gain perspective. If people will think, they can foresee and weigh the likely consequences of their potential actions.

Notice how God offers Cain hope and encouragement. "If you do well, will you not be accepted?" (Gen 4:6) God is saying, "This is nowhere near hopeless. You have not destroyed your life. No door has been permanently closed. Your destiny is still within your control. You still have choices, good choices. You can still do right and reap the rewards."

When people err in public, they often feel an extra sting. Everybody saw. Everybody knows. I've been judged. I'll always be judged. Life is broken beyond repair. It doesn't matter what I do next. I'm ruined. In such situations, there's tremendous power in offering hope. The Bible utterly rejects fatalism.

The offer must be both legitimate and realistic, but God makes that so much easier for us. Looking forward in Scripture, we see a murdering adulterer forgiven and allowed to serve as king. We see a denier preaching on Pentecost. We see a persecutor appointed as apostle to the Gentiles. One of our greatest roles in helping people is extending hope and reminding people of God's power to forgive.

Not only does God extend an offer of help, pose great questions, and offer hope, but He also offers Cain a spiritual perspective on his situation. In this regard, church leaders who try to help others stand firmly with God. "If you do not do well, sin is crouching at the door" (Gen 4:7). We can't read that line from the ESV without remembering 1 Peter 5:8, "Be sober-minded, be watchful. Your adversary the devil prowls around like a roaring lion, seeking someone to devour." Crouching or prowling, this evil lion plans to eat.

Again, there's no fatalism. God says of sin, "Its desire is for you, but you must rule over it" (Gen 4:7). What a statement! "You must rule over it" necessarily implies that you can rule over it. With God's help, you have the strength, wisdom, and insight. Don't cave. Step up. Make the Godward choice. What a message of hope and faith!

How were God's efforts repaid? You know how the story ends. "Cain rose up against his brother Abel and killed him" (Gen 4:8). Cain rejected God's counsel, committed murder, and then tried to cover his sin. God did not fail Cain; Cain failed both God and himself. Cain received perfect counsel and rejected it. He did the very opposite of what God taught him.

These facts hold tremendous power for every Christian who tries to help others. God rightly holds us responsible for our attitudes, words, and actions. The Lord does not hold us responsible for people's responses to our godly efforts. This is clearly taught in the famous watchman passage, Ezekiel 33. It's just as clearly exemplified in Jesus's encounter with the rich young ruler. The young man did not leave in sorrow because Jesus failed him. He left in pain because he failed to live up to what he knew to be true (Mark 10:17–22). When it comes to helping people, what counts is faithful, loving effort rather than the ultimate result. If we cannot accept this truth, we won't last long as people helpers. If we try to bear the responsibility of others, we will crumble under the irrational load.

# God with Job

Job is an astonishingly difficult story. Why would the Lord point out Job to His evil adversary (Job 1:8)? Why would God allow Satan to take so much from Job? Why would God allow Job's friends (frenemies?) to be so stunningly wrong in their assessment of Job's situation? What right do I have as a creature, finite and flawed, to question the Almighty?

Sometimes God doesn't tell us all that we want to know. In Job's case, He doesn't offer even a hint of an answer. On the plus side are two key statements: Even facing cataclysmic loss, "In all this Job did not sin or charge God with wrong" (Job 1:22). And in one of Scripture's fiercest statements of faith, "Though He slay me, I will hope in Him ..." (Job 13:15).

On the other side of the coin, even Job makes major assumptions that do not serve him well. Half of Job 13:15 is quoted above. The other half states, "... yet I will argue my ways to His face." Job believes that God owes him an answer. Job believes that he would be blessed in some way if God would just explain Himself. To his credit, Job pivots to humble repentance when God falsifies his assumptions (Job 38:1–42:6, especially 40:3–5 and 42:1–6).

What does Job teach us about efforts to help people? Far more happens in the unseen realms than we know or understand (Job 1–2, Eph 6:12). Sometimes our lifelong friends can be miserable counselors, making horrible assumptions (Job 4:7). Sometimes we deceive ourselves by thinking, "If I only knew why this was happening, I could bear it better." Any of us can fall into the trap of imagining that God owes us answers. There may be answers that we're incapable of processing even if they were clearly stated. The reasons behind great loss do nothing to quell the pain of that loss.

What implications for counseling can church leaders draw from the story of Job? Watch our assumptions. Practice humility. Only God always knows the whole story.

Don't speak where God is silent. Don't say more than we know to be true. Let God be God. Don't go beyond the word.

Sometimes, silence is the very best course of action (Job 2:11–13). There are problems we can't solve. There are problems that defy solutions. There are questions that can't be answered. There are needs that we can't meet, no matter how much we try or how deeply we love. To quote the great philosopher Clint Eastwood, "A man's got to know his limitations."

In the end, God blesses the faithful. God always does right. God is always trustworthy. God is always God. We trust God based on His self-revelation. Sometimes, we find ourselves trusting God because there's no other sensible choice. Though He loves us and constantly draws near, there is no gulf in the universe as great as the gulf between creature and Creator. We are incapable of understanding how great He is and how limited we are.

Job's bottom line for us: Don't try to explain the inexplicable. Don't say more than God reveals. Never blame the victim. Revere God even in the darkest of times.

## God with David

After David's greatest set of sins, God sent the prophet Nathan to his lost and damaged king. While Nathan mouths the words, he speaks God's truth in 2 Samuel 12. The key element of this encounter is truth-telling through narrative, using story and metaphor to speak to the heart.

We feel sorry for Nathan on this mission. He could be killed for confronting his king. To Nathan's credit, when God sends, he goes. It's an outstanding example of courage. Is it also a reminder that we need not desire or delight in the mission God gives us? People helping isn't always easy or pleasant. As servants of God and doers of good, our job is to hear God and obey.

We know the famous story of the horrible rich man and the poor man's pet lamb. We understand why this story is perfect for David. He has risked his life to protect sheep that, to the best of our knowledge, were never "like a daughter to him" (1 Sam 17:33–37). Think of all the psalms where David speaks of shepherd and sheep, none more famous than Psalm 23 (Ps 78:70–72, Ps 79:13, Ps 95:6–7, Ps 100:3).

What are the implications for church leaders who counsel? Clearly, we recognize the power of metaphor and story. We recognize the power of speaking to both the head and the heart. We remember that the most direct approach isn't always the best approach. We see that helping sinful people confront themselves is far superior when our goal is repentance and restoration.

Even when we are blessed to bring people to the cusp of life-changing insight, we must summon the courage to take the next step, to clearly say what God would have us say. Nathan excels in courage and clarity (2 Sam 12:7–12). We don't think of him as gloating, but he doesn't mince words. We don't see him as reveling in the moment when he gave a king his comeuppance. We see him as God's instrument doing all that he can to "save a soul from death and cover a multitude of sins" (Jas 5:19–20). We see him doing God's merciful work, snatching a soul out of the fire (Jude 22–23).

## God with Elijah

We will reserve 1 Kings 19, one of Scripture's classic people-helping encounters, for the chapter "Helping the Depressed." (Pages 137–146 in *Counseling for Church Leaders: A Practical Guide*. Bill Bagents and Rosemary Snodgrass. Florence, AL: Heritage Christian University Press, 2021). Please note that it powerfully fits this chapter as well. For a well-considered alternate view of 1 Kings 19 see Ed Gallagher's essay "A Still Small Voice" (Pages 88–105 in *Fighting the Good Fight: A Festschrift for Bill Bagents*. Editors of Heritage Christian University Press. Florence, AL: Heritage Christian University Press, 2022).

# God with His Chosen People

We include a discussion of Isaiah 1 because it, like Nathan's confrontation with David, presents the teaching aspect of God's corrective counsel being offered. It does not employ a heartrending story. Rather, it features clear, direct presentation of facts with both powerful metaphors and a strong emphasis on the consequences of sinful actions. It's logical and cognitive to the core. There's no beating around the bush, no mincing of words. Both lives and souls are at stake.

God's people have rebelled (Isa 1:2). Even the ox and the donkey don't forget their masters, but God's people have forgotten (Isa 1:3). God's people have broken faith with Him (Isa 1:4). And they are reaping terrible consequences (Isa 1:5–9). They still observe religious rituals, but those acts hold no meaning for God (Isa 1:10–15). As bad as things are, the situation isn't hopeless. Repentance and restoration are possible (Isa 1:16–17). Think. Consider your ways. You're on the path to death and destruction. Choose life with God (Isa 41:18–20).

Are there occasions when church leaders must be this blunt when offering help to others? Yes. We suggest the following implications from Isaiah 1. While not fans of Dr. Phil's practice of televising the struggles of vulnerable people, we appreciate the wisdom of his trademark question: "How's that working out for you?" That's the question God asks through Isaiah. "Can't you see what's happening to you?" "Do you call your present state of affairs desirable?" "Do you want to continue down this path?" "Can't you see that it ends in death?"

These questions aren't threats. They're stout calls to realistic assessment. "Please stop pretending." "End the denial." "There's no path forward until we get real."

Note that God clearly presents a reality check, but He tempers its stoutness with hope. He reminds His people that they can choose their behavior—that they have superior options (Isa 1:5). Things don't have to continue as they are. He reminds them that He can neither accept their worship nor hear their prayers as they continue in rebellion (Isa 1:11–15). He also invites them to wash themselves and make themselves clean, to learn to do good again (Isa 1:16–17).

No matter how far people fall, we don't fall outside the reach of God's grace. As long as there is breath, there is hope. That's one of the highest motivations for helping people in the name of God. He can forgive any sin that we will renounce. He can restore any trust that we break. He takes no delight in the death of the wicked (Ezek 33:11). His will has always been to save rather than to destroy (John 3:16–17, 1 Tim 2:3–6).

Yes, this is an unapologetic appeal to church leaders to reach out to the rebellious, to both those who are aggressive/hostile and those who are passive/unaware. We offer four reasons. Doing so reflects what God has done for us; it follows God's example (Rom 5:6–8). Doing so makes us obedient servants of God (2 Cor 5:13–21, 1 Tim 2:3–5). As in Isaiah's day, a faithful remnant will hear and answer.

Some will choose to be reconciled to God. Finally, even if most don't welcome our efforts, we'll be better for having tried.

## Objections to the Concept of God as Counselor

"It's both presumptuous and blasphemous to present God as 'The First and Greatest Therapist.'" We intend no such presentation. The focus of this book isn't therapy. Our focus is choosing to help people draw near to God and live better in Christ by showing them the love of God and the wisdom of living God's way. God is love, God loves people, and love acts to bless people.

"Intervening in people's lives, aka meddling in their business, is fine for God. He's the Creator. He's all-knowing. He never errs. We often err. We need to leave people-helping to Him." The most effective deceptions contain maximum statements of truth. God is perfect, infinitely superior to us in every way. Yet, God lives in us and works through us. God commissions us to love and do good works (Gal 6:10, Eph 2:10, Titus 2:7 & 14, 3:8 & 14). We are instructed to "look to the interests of others" (Phil 2:4) and to "bear one another's burdens" (Gal 6:2).

"We'll never be able to perfectly imitate God's love." That's true. We also won't be able to perfectly imitate His holiness, but that's still the standard taught by Scripture (1 Pet 1:13–16). His love remains both our motivation and our standard (1 John 4:9–11). Our love for God merits more than our best effort. It also merits every effort to make our best better. We keep adding skills, wisdom, knowledge, and spiritual maturity so we'll be ever more able to serve God and His people. Even at our best, we maintain the perspective and humility of Luke 17:5–10, but we take great heart in the fact that God allows us to serve in His name and to His glory.

## Note

This chapter first appeared as "God as Counselor." Pages 12–22 in *Counseling for Church Leaders: A Practical Guide*. Bill Bagents and Rosemary Snodgrass. Heritage Christian Leadership Institute Series. Florence, AL: Heritage Christian University Press, 2021.

# Chapter 3

## *God's Comfort*
### Isaiah 40

## Focus Passage

Isaiah 40:28–31

## One Main Thing

God delights in comforting and strengthening His beloved people.

## Introduction

Isaiah 40 sings and soars as it extols the breadth and beauty of God's comfort for those who love Him. We cannot imagine a richer description of God's goodness toward His people. And we find this amazing in a book that so stoutly documents the fierce costs of sin.

The Book of Isaiah begins and ends with the reality of Israel's rebellion.

> Hear, O heavens, and give ear, earth; for the Lord has spoken: Children have I reared and brought up, but they have rebelled against me. The ox knows its owner, and the donkey its master's crib, but Israel does not know; my people do not understand (Isa 1:2–3).

> And they shall go out and look on the dead bodies of the men who have rebelled against me. For their worm shall not die, their fire shall not be quenched, and they shall be an abhorrence to all flesh (Isa 66:24).

As if these bookends were not sufficient, Isaiah 39:5–8 records God's promise of judgment to King Hezekiah. The bottom line is striking: Babylon will come and "Nothing shall be left ... ." Terrible days lie ahead.

Despite Israel's faithlessness, all is not lost. For all the just judgment and stout rebuke within this book, there remains a clear theme of hope, comfort, and redemption for the remnant who choose to love and trust God. Nowhere is that theme clearer than in Isaiah 40.

## Going Deeper

Isaiah 40 begins with a shout of hope! God commissions His prophet to break out a message of comfort that flows from His majesty and extols His might. It tenderly expresses God's faithful love, offering amazing joy to all "who wait on the Lord" (Isa 40:31).

Isaiah clearly documents God's grace toward His people. Their comfort doesn't come because God has changed His nature or forgotten their sins. It comes on the heels of righteous judgment and offers new life.

The poetry of Isaiah 40:3–8 grasps both head and heart. A new way and a new day are coming. Paths will be made level and straight so that all can see the glory of the Lord. All must see that God has not forgotten His people.

Isaiah masterfully contrasts the greatness of God with the smallness and fragility of His people (Isa 40:6–30). The scope and clarity remind us of Job 38–41. "All flesh is grass, and all its beauty like the flower of the field" (Isa 40:6–7). It's gone in a breath. "But the word of the Lord will stand forever" (Isa 40:8). The contrast is clear, but it is in no sense negative. Rather, it sets up the momentous good news that comes next.

God is coming to claim His people. He's coming with His army "and his reward is with him" (Isa 40:10). He's coming for relief and deliverance. He's coming like a shepherd to care for His flock. His tenderness is matched by His awesome power.

Who can measure earth's waters in the hollow of His hand? Who can measure the heavens in a span? Who can weigh the mountains? Who can offer counsel to the Omniscient One? Combine the wealth, wisdom, power, and talent of all the nations, and they're "like a drop from a bucket" or "dust on the scales" compared to the Almighty (Isa 40:15).

Ever the Teacher, God has His prophet include a warning against idolatry, particularly against violating the second commandment of Exodus 20:4–6 (Isa 40:19–20). The Lord is too majestic to be represented by any creation of a human, even if that creation flows from a master craftsman using silver and gold. The inanimate cannot represent the ultimate Mover, the force that both created and sustains all life.

Compared to God, we are but insects (Isa 40:22). Even if a prince established a dynasty, his fleeting moment of power is less than a moment to God (Isa 40:24). Creature has no standing to question the Creator. Creature has no way to hide action, motive, or thought from the Creator (Isa 40:37–38). Creature certainly has no right to complain that the Creator has disregarded his rights or delayed his deliverance.

Isaiah's contrast between those who demand an answer from their Creator and those who choose to trust Him stands both subtle and strong. The magnificent Creator, the everlasting God, never grows faint or weary (Isa 40:28). And He never falls petty or small. The Almighty soars in grace and love as He gives power and strength to the weak (Isa 40:29). This power exceeds human imagination. If we think of it in terms of the fittest youth in prime of life, we have not touched the hem of the garment (Isa 40:30). It's not about physical prowess or athletic endurance. It's not about physical or mental stamina. In soaring climax, only poetic language can convey the spiritual reality of Isaiah 40.

> ... They who wait for the Lord shall renew their strength; they shall mount up with wings like eagles; they shall run and not be weary; they shall walk and not faint (Isa 40:31).

Who, but God, could make such a promise to a people who were about to be ground to dust by 70 years of oppression? Who, but God, would know the power of a promise to fill hurting hearts with soul-sustaining hope? Who, but God, would dare to love so fully?

## Application

We read Isaiah 40 through the lens of Romans 15:4 and 1 Corinthians 10:11. We believe that those ancient words remain God's word to His people in every generation. In many respects, the bridge of application between Isaiah's first hearers and us is remarkably short.

God has always been "the Father of mercies and God of all comfort" (2 Cor 1:3). The Lord has an amazing history of commissioning His servants to comfort the afflicted (John 14:1–3, 1 Thess 4:13–18, Rev 21:1–4). Two thoughts immediately come to mind. We are doing God's work God's way whenever we offer legitimate biblical comfort to others. In doing so, we stand in a long and loving tradition of faithful service. Secondly, each of us has received amazing comfort from God, through both Scripture and the kind words of those who are taught and motivated by Scripture.

Isaiah 40 also reminds us that the comfort of God comes with content. As powerful as God's word stands, God's word is never "just words." It flows from, and is, truth. When the voice said, "Cry!" Isaiah asked the perfect question: "What shall I cry?" (Isa 40:6) Isaiah knew he needed to communicate spiritual content, God's truth, if he was to bless his people. That principle will stand as long as this earth stands.

Isaiah 40 reminds us that God does not comfort His people while they persist in rebellion. He does not comfort us in our sins. He comforts us when we renounce sin, amend our ways, and return to faithfulness (Isa 40:1–2). As much as God loves to comfort, He never deceives. Sin costs. It always costs more than advertised.

Isaiah 40 powerfully reminds us of the omniscience of God. He is always prepared to bless, save, rescue, and grow His people. Isaiah 40:3–5 reminds the people of God to prepare to see and to receive His blessings. God can create amazing new days for people who have the faith to receive them.

In many respects, Isaiah 40 is best read in concert with Isaiah 6, the prophet's vision of the throne of God. We know the ancient truism, "Get God right, and you'll get life right." Seeing God's power and purity, God's majesty and might, God's grace and God's goodness, sets the stage for faithful living. He knows all, so we need to ask Him to teach us. He has all power, so we ask Him to aid us. He is the ultimate leader, so we gladly follow. A huge message from Isaiah 40 is "let God be God." Our salvation is not in human wisdom, wealth, education, government, or technology. God alone is worthy of adoration and complete trust. No idol of any type must be allowed to distract us from the majesty of God.

## Conclusion

Isaiah 40 is an amazing song of spiritual success. It's a sweet and powerful declaration of God's fierce love. It's a moving reminder that God comforts and saves those who trust Him. It's a clear declaration that God's comfort is far more than the mere endurance of barely hanging on by a thread. Ultimately, God's comfort ends in soaring strength. God's comfort ends in salvation. It ends in the peace that passes understanding. It ends with us at home with Him forever.

## Discussion Questions

1. In what ways has God offered comfort to you and your family? In what ways does He continue to do so?
2. In what ways has God blessed you to offer hope and comfort to others?

3. What can we do to heighten our appreciation for the majesty of God?

4. How will it bless us to better grasp the majesty of God?

5. In what ways and through what means does God renew the strength of His people today?

6. Why does God continue to renew the strength of those who serve Him?

## Note

This chapter first appeared as "God's Comfort: Isaiah 40." Pages 79–86 in *Mercy and Majesty: God Through the Eyes of Isaiah*. Berean Bible Study Series. Edited by Bill Bagents. Florence, AL: Heritage Christian University Press, 2022.

# Chapter 4

## *God Is Omnipresent*

The Bible teaches that God stands outside the limitations of time and space. In that "God is Spirit" (John 4:24), He is not bound by laws of physics. Nowhere is this doctrine taught more clearly than in Psalm 139. Linking the concepts of God's omniscience and omnipotence, Psalm 139 begins by asserting that God understands our thoughts before we complete them, He comprehends our motives before we translate them into action, and He even knows our words before we speak them. In the words of Jeremiah 20:12, God "sees the mind and heart."

Concerning God's omnipresence, Psalm 139:7 asks, "Where can I go from your Spirit? Or where can I flee from Your presence?" It is not that the psalmist wants to flee God's presence. Rather, he is celebrating the fact that God will always be with him no matter where he goes. From the highest heaven to the underworld, the psalmist says to God, "You are there!" David anticipates such teaching in Psalm 23:4: "Even though I walk through the valley of the shadow of death, I will fear no evil, for you are with me; your rod and your staff, they comfort me." If wings could fly the psalmist to the uttermost parts of the sea, God is there. Darkness or light, God is present. The Bible presents God as eyewitness to every action in every place at all times. Nothing is hidden from His sight.

The doctrine of God's omnipresence is taught in many places in the Bible. Jeremiah 23:23–24 reads,

> "Am I a God at hand," declares the Lord, "and not a God far away? Can a man hide himself in secret places so that I cannot see him?" declares the Lord. "Do I not fill heaven and earth?" declares the Lord.

God first spoke these words to false prophets who claimed to speak in His name. He used these questions to document the futility of their actions. How can one think that his words will go unnoticed if the God of heaven is everywhere at all times? From the perspective of the righteous, 1 Peter 3:12 quotes Psalm 34:15: "For the eyes of the Lord are on the righteous, and His ears are open to their prayer." The Bible teaches that the eyes of the Lord are always on the righteous, and His ears are always open to their prayers. The Bible presents God as one who will never leave nor forsake His people (Heb 13:5).

In addition to such direct statements, the Bible also dramatically asserts God's omnipresence through many strong, but less direct statements. Concerning our words, Matthew 12:36 records the teaching of Jesus: "I tell you, on the day of judgment people will give account for every careless word they speak." That statement assumes God's omnipresence. How else could God know every word that men speak? Consider Hagar and Ishmael as they were sent away from Abraham's camp. When they fell into distress in the wilderness, "And God heard the voice of the boy," (Gen 21:17). God heard because He was present to hear!

When Jesus asks, "Are not five sparrows sold for two pennies? And not one of them is forgotten before God," He implies the omnipresence of God (Luke 12:6). When Jesus says, "Why even the hairs of your head are all numbered," He implies both God's omniscience and His omnipresence (Luke 12:7). More than that, He reminds us of God's ongoing personal concern for His creation.

When Jesus speaks of doing charitable deeds, praying, and fasting secretly so as to bring glory to God, He uses identical phrases in describing God's blessings: "... And your Father who sees in secret will reward you" (Matt 6:4, 6, and 18). God not only sees in the secret place, *He is in the secret place.* Because of His omnipresence, He is eyewitness to every good deed that we do.

When Jesus promises, "For where two or three are gathered in my name, there am I among them," He is not speaking poetically (Matt 18:20). Rather, He is speaking prophetically. When Jesus ascended from earth to return to the Father, He resumed all the attributes of deity. He resumed omnipresence, allowing Him to be with His people in all places at all times. Thus, His promise at the ascension, "... And behold, I am with you always, to the end of the age" (Matt 28:20).

Concerning the great and final day of judgment, the apostle Paul writes, "For we must all appear before the judgment seat of Christ, that each one may receive the things done in the body, according to what he has done, whether good or bad" (2 Cor 5:10). The passage assumes that God knows all that has been done, thereby implying His omnipresence. The point is even stronger in Luke 8:17, as Jesus says, "For nothing is hidden that will not be made manifest, nor is anything secret that will not be known and come to light." God knows our conduct because He is ever present to observe it.

## Apparent Contradictions

Students of the Bible have asked, "If God is present everywhere at all times, then why does the Bible speak of God's coming and going, His arrival and departure?" Genesis 3 records important, tragic interaction between Eve and the serpent. As part of that interaction, both Eve and Adam sin. Guilt and fear enter their hearts for the first time. Where is God when this is happening? More than that, Genesis 3:8 mentions Adam and Eve hearing

> the sound of the Lord God walking in the garden in the
> cool of the day, and the man and his wife hid themselves

from the presence of the Lord God among the trees of
the garden.

Sometimes, questions are best answered by questions.
Does the fact that the presence of God is not mentioned
earlier in Genesis 3 prove that He was absent? Does the
fact that God allowed Adam and Eve to perceive the
sound of His movement in the garden prove that God was
incapable of silent movement? Does the fact that Adam
and Eve attempted to hide from God's presence prove that
such is possible? Though the Lord spoke to them, asking,
"Where are you?" could He not have done so to give them
opportunity to respond and begin a conversation?

Many times the Bible speaks of God appearing to
people. Some have asserted that this language implies that
God is not omnipresent. For example, Genesis 17:1
records God's appearance to Abram to reaffirm His
covenant. Genesis 18:1 records that the Lord appeared to
Abraham using the form of three men. The biblical
doctrine of God's omnipresence does not assert that God
is always visible to the human eye. Quite the contrary,
even within the Bible direct visible manifestations of
God's presence are rare. Such manifestations are reserved
for occasions of special commission, encouragement, or
communication. Reports of God's visible, dramatic presence do not deny the doctrine of His omnipresence
throughout the world.

In Psalm 51:11, a heartbroken and penitent David
pleads with God in these words, "Cast me not away from

your presence, and take not your Holy Spirit from me."
Thus, the question, "If God is omnipresent, how could
David fear that God would cast him away from His presence? How can a person be cast from the presence of an
omnipresent being?"

The Bible recognizes different levels or types of
God's presence. From a general perspective, God is
everywhere and all is within His presence. From a relational perspective, only those who walk with God on His
terms are deemed worthy to live in His presence. Recognizing this truth, Psalm 15:1 asks, "O Lord, who shall
sojourn in Your tent? Who may dwell on your holy
hill?" A series of moral and ethical answers follows.
Only the person who walks blamelessly, does what is
right, speaks truth in his heart, avoids slander, does no
evil, opposes evil people, and keeps his word can live
with God. Psalm 24:3 asks virtually the same question
and gives a shorter version of the same answer. The full
blessings of God's presence are reserved for those whose
lives honor Him.

## Philosophical and Logical Challenges to Omnipresence

Thoughtful students have asked, "If God is omnipresent,
then tell me how evil exists. How do so many terrible
things happen if God is everywhere?" Students of the
Bible do not deny the presence and power of evil in this
world. For example, Cain killed his brother, Abel (Gen 4).

God saw this conflict coming. He intervened, asking Cain three excellent questions:

- "Why are you angry?"
- "And why has your face fallen?"
- "If you do well, will you not be accepted?"

God said to Cain, "And if you do not do well, sin is crouching at the door. Its desire is contrary to you, but you must rule over it" (Gen 4:7). God did not remove Cain's ability to choose his actions. In that God allowed Cain to control his own behavior, God's presence and intervention did not prevent the murder of Abel.

Similarly, as Stephen was being opposed by a religious mob, he saw "the heavens opened and the Son of Man standing at the right hand of God" (Acts 7:56). Rather than leading to Stephen's protection or the repentance of the mob, Stephen's description of what he saw infuriated them to the point of murder. Even direct perception of the presence of God did not change the physical reality of Stephen's situation. In a world where God allows people to choose their actions, God's presence does not overrule their behavior.

## Classic Misunderstandings of God's Omnipresence

Some affirm God's omnipresence from a non-biblical perspective. Some have reasoned, "Certainly, God is present everywhere and at all times. This is obvious because all that we see is God. There is no distinction between Creator and creation. All is one in seamless unity." Others take a more moderate position, affirming, "Certainly, God is present everywhere and at all times. This has to be true because there is something of God in everything that God has made." These statements do not agree with the biblical doctrine of the omnipresence of God.

Clearly, Bible teaches that God created all that exists. The Bible begins with these words, "In the beginning, God created the heavens and the earth" (Gen 1:1). Psalm 19:1 adds, "The heavens declare the glory of God, and the sky above shows His handiwork." Colossians 1:15–17 says of Jesus Christ,

> He is the image of the invisible God, the firstborn over all creation. For by him all things were created, in heaven and on earth, visible and invisible, whether thrones or dominions or rulers or authorities—all things were created through him and for him. And he is before all things, and in him all things hold together.

Hebrews 1:1–2 speaks of Jesus Christ as God's "Son, whom he appointed the heir of all things, through whom also he created the world."

While God made the world and loves His creation, the Bible recognizes a strong and consistent distinction between the Creator and His creation. The Bible never asserts that every aspect of creation is somehow divine, containing something that is God. Of all creation, only humanity is said to be created in the image of God (Gen 1:26–27). Even affirming that fact, the Bible still recognizes the dramatic difference between the Creator and His creation. Psalm 95:6–7 pleasantly urges, "Oh come, let us worship and bow down; let us kneel before the Lord our Maker! For He is our God, and we are the people of his pasture, and the sheep of His hand." Though He honored us by making us in His image, "a little lower than the heavenly beings and crowned him with glory and honor" (Ps 8:5), we pale in comparison to God (Jer 10:23 and Job 37–41). As taught in Isaiah 55:8–9,

> For my thoughts are not your thoughts, neither are your
> ways my ways, declares the Lord. For as the heavens are
> higher than the earth, so are my ways higher than your
> ways, and my thoughts than your thoughts.

While God made the world and loves His creation, He tells us that His creation is not permanent. God intends to take the faithful home to heaven. Of this earth, 2 Peter 3:10 says,

> But the day of the Lord will come like a thief, and then
> the heavens will pass away with a roar, and the heavenly
> bodies will be burned up and dissolved. and the earth
> and the works that are done on it will be exposed.

The physical universe will be destroyed, but the spiritual universe endures forever.

From a Christian perspective, some have proposed that the omnipresence of God guarantees that nothing truly evil or damaging will ever happen to a faithful believer. They assert that passages including Romans 8:31–39 and Ephesians 3:20–21 guarantee God's ongoing protection from all types of harm. Sadly, they fail to see that Romans 8:35 acknowledges that Christians can face tribulation, distress, persecution, famine, nakedness, danger, and sword. They fail to remember that Paul was in prison when he wrote the letter to the Ephesians. They fail to remember the many negative challenges that Paul endured for the sake of the gospel (2 Cor 11:22–28). They fail to remember the direct statements of 1 Peter 2:19–20, that one can endure "sorrows while suffering unjustly" and one can "do good and suffer for it." While we greatly appreciate the fact that God stands with His people in all their trials, His omnipresence does not shield Christians from all trials.

## What Difference Does the Omnipresence of God Make to Me?

Some view the omnipresence of God negatively. They think of the concept as being spied upon and having their privacy violated. The Bible never presents the omnipresence of God in such terms. In fact, the Bible warns against the danger of forgetting the omniscience and omnipresence of God. Psalm 10:8–13 describes an evil person who lurks in secret places as he plots theft and murder. Verse 11 details the flawed thinking that leads the evil person to such actions. "He says in his heart, 'God has forgotten, he has hidden his face, He will never see it.'" Psalm 94:4–7 echoes this thought. The wicked speak insolently, afflict God's people, and even resort to murder, saying, "The Lord does not see; the God of Jacob does not perceive." This error is so grave that the next verse labels those who espouse it "dullest of the people" and "fools" (Ps 94:8). What a dangerous state in which to live!

Christians welcome the omnipresence of God as an act of homage and submission. The psalm that speaks most directly to God's omnipresence ends with these words, "Search me, O God, and know my heart! Try me and know my thoughts. And see if there is any grievous way in me, and lead me in the way everlasting" (Ps 139:23–24)! The psalmist welcomes God's presence and God's complete knowledge of his heart and life. He trusts God with his life and his soul. As Acts 17:28 acknowledges, "'In Him we live and move and have our being'; as even some of our own poets have said, 'For we are indeed his offspring.'" In the words of Psalm 100:3, "Know that the Lord, he is God! It is he who has made us, and we are his. We are his people and the sheep of his pasture." Because God is creator and sustainer, He has every right to be present in our lives. Because God is gracious and loving, we want Him to be present with us every moment.

Christians view the omnipresence of God as one of

His greatest blessings, a tremendous manifestation of grace. Belief in the omnipresence of God provides many benefits to God's people.

God's presence acts as a deterrent to sin. If God is everywhere and knows all, there is no provision for hiding sin. "... Be sure your sin will find you out" stands as a barrier to willful, rebellious sin (Num 32:23b). Loyalty to God, the fact that he hates sin, and the knowledge that He sees all strongly encourage righteousness. We see this in the life of Joseph. When tempted by Potiphar's wife, Joseph's refusal was accompanied by these words, "How then can I do this great wickedness and sin against God?" (Gen 39:9)

God's presence ensures that no good deed will go unnoticed. As noted above, this is clearly taught in Matthew 6:1, 4, 6, and 18. Matthew 10:40–42 records a promise of reward stated by Jesus. It ends by saying, "And whoever gives one of these little ones even a cup of cold water because he is a disciple, truly, I say to you, he shall by no means lose his reward." God's omnipresence guarantees that every good work is known and appreciated by God. In Matthew 25:34–40, Jesus declares that He takes such works personally: "Assuredly I say to you, inasmuch as you did it to one of the least of these My brethren, you did it to Me."

God's omnipresence ensures that the Christian is never alone as he or she endures temptation or stress. Hebrews 13:5 uses God's words of Deuteronomy 31:6 and 8, "I will never leave you nor forsake you." Hebrews 13:6

reads, "So we can confidently say, 'The Lord is my helper; I will not fear; what can man do to me?'" Paul echoes this concept in Philippians 4:13: "I can do all things through him who strengthens me." In the context of Philippians 4, "do" means "endure" or "overcome."

God's omnipresence offers spiritual and emotional comfort to the believer. In the language of the shepherd, David says, "Even though I walk through the valley of the shadow of death, I will fear no evil, for you are with me; your rod and your staff, they comfort me" (Ps 23:4). In Psalm 145:17–20, David adds,

> The Lord is righteous in all his ways and kind in all his works. The Lord is near to all who call upon him, to all who call upon him in truth. He fulfills the desire of those who fear him; he also hears their cry and saves them. The Lord preserves all who love him ...

Many biblical examples prove that God's preservation of those who love Him may be spiritual salvation rather than protection here on earth. No matter the level of protection, the comfort of God's presence is real.

God's omnipresence means that God is always available to hear our prayers. This gift is not to be accepted presumptuously. Rather, it is a precious blessing. 1 Peter 3:12 quotes Psalm 34:15–16: "For the eyes of the Lord are on the righteous, and his ears are open to their prayers; but the face of the Lord is against those who do evil." The privilege of being heard favorably by God is directly linked both to our conduct and our faith (1 Pet 3:8–12 and Jas 1:5–8). God's ability to hear the prayers of all the faithful is compelling evidence of His power and majesty. God's willingness to be present with His children and to care for us is equally compelling evidence of His goodness and His grace.

## Conclusion

The Bible clearly teaches that God is omnipresent (Ps 139:7–12). This truth is taught through numerous proofs, both direct and indirect. The willingness of God to be near to us demonstrates His love and concern. The blessings of His presence are greater than our ability to state or comprehend. God's omnipresence calls on us to live consistently in the light of His love and truth. It offers us a foretaste of life in heaven where we will see Him face to face forever.

## Note

This chapter first appeared as "God Is Omnipresent." Pages 83–96 in *I AM: A Study of the True and Living God*. Edited by Jeremy W. Barrier and Charles R. Webb. Florence, AL: Heritage Press: Florence, 2010.

# Chapter 5

## *God's Responses to Human Complaints*

A dmittedly, this essay takes a broad view of human complaints, allowing the phrase to include complaints, objections, resistance, accusations, and requests for accommodation. Under that broad umbrella, we find both the frequency and variety of complaints against the Almighty within the Bible to be amazing. And sad. And informative. And worthy of investigation.

The Bible leaves no doubt as to the first recorded complaint against God. In Genesis 3:1–5, the serpent first planted a seed of doubt: "Did God actually say, 'You shall not eat of any tree in the garden'?" He immediately moved to denying God's integrity and impugning His motives— "You will not surely die. For God knows when you eat of it your eyes will be opened, and you will be like God, knowing good and evil." Thus, the story of the fall. Satan complained against God, Eve came to believe the complaint, and Adam joined in the sin.

## The First Family

It takes little creativity to read Genesis 3:8–13 as a set of complaints against God. Caught by both his actions and his words, Adam infamously said, "The woman whom you gave to be with me, she gave me, and I ate." Eve continued, "The serpent deceived me, and I ate." And who created the serpent? Who allowed the serpent access to Eve? Who allowed the serpent a voice?

God's response to this initial set of complaints is, in a sense, a non-response. The text offers no record of God addressing Adam and Eve's attempts at blame-shifting. Could it be that both He and they knew these frivolous attempts merited no denial? From a different perspective, God responded in a stunning way to their complaints. He put them out of the garden, denied them access to the tree of life, and allowed them to face new struggles and challenges. God let them bear the cost of their rebellion. He extended grace by allowing them to live, clothing them, and blessing them with children; but He also remained true to His just and holy nature. In doing so, He taught us that sin always exacts a cost.

Genesis 4 offers an even clearer example of a complaint against God. Despite God's clear warning and offer of hope, Cain murdered his brother. As God imposed the sentence of agricultural failure and life as a "fugitive and a wanderer on the earth," Cain infamously complained, "My punishment is more than I can bear."

He added, "And whoever finds me will kill me." Under the law stated in Genesis 9:6, Cain deserved that fate.

What was God's response to Cain's complaint? Remarkable grace: "And the Lord put a mark on Cain lest any who found him should attack him" (Gen 4:15). God extended protection to a man who deserved none, while at the same time standing by the sentence He imposed. Within the first pages of scripture, we find two outstanding examples of judgment tempered by mercy.

## Abraham and Family

We have the greatest respect for Abraham as the father of the faithful and the friend of God. We also acknowledge that he was just as human as the rest of us. Abraham and Sarah waited twenty-five years for the promise of Genesis 12:3, "I will make of you a great nation," until the birth of Isaac. We marvel at their faith and love. We take heart in their inclusion in Hebrews 11 as powerful examples of faith. And we know that they complained to God—multiple times.

"But Abram said, 'O Lord God, what will you give me, for I continue childless ...'" (Gen 15:2). "Behold, you have given me no offspring" (Gen 15:3). The Lord offered three responses to these questions/complaints. He reiterated His promise of a son and heirs like "the number of the stars" (Gen 15:4–5). Second, God repeated His land promise to Abram and commanded Abram to offer a series of sacrifices in recognition of God's covenant with him.

Finally, He spoke to Abram through a dream confirming His promise (Gen 15:12–16).

Is it unfair or fanciful to think of Abram and Sarai's plot to have an heir through Hagar as a complaint against God (Gen 16)? Clearly, the Lord rejected their plan. Just as clearly, the Lord preserved the lives of Hagar and Ishmael and allowed a powerful nation to descend from Abraham's first son (Gen 17:20).

At age 99, God again affirmed His plan to give Abram and Sarai a son and to build their descendants into a great nation (Gen 17). Abram believed God and confirmed his faith by instituting the covenant of circumcision. Both Abram and Sarai accepted the new names that God gave them. But even after those noble expressions of faith, "Abraham fell on his face and laughed and said to himself, 'Shall a child be born to a man who is a hundred years old? Shall Sarah, who is ninety years old bear a child?'" (Gen 17:17) Sarah later expressed her doubts similarly (Gen 18:12–15).

How did God respond to these doubts and frustrations? He repeated His promise with one additional detail, "I will surely return to you about this time next year, and Sarah your wife shall have a son" (Gen 18:10). Though the Lord has no obligation to repeat Himself, He often does for our benefit and comfort. We see yet another powerful example of patience, mercy, and grace.

# Job

The suffering and endurance of Job are legendary. In the end of the story, Job confessed God's greatness and was restored to health, wealth, and respect. Job's trials, however, provided unimaginable challenges.

Job's three friends shared a common belief: terrible suffering and loss do not afflict people who are faithful to God (Job 4:7–11, 8:1–7, 11:1–6). To the best of our knowledge, they knew nothing of the events recorded in Job 1–2. They were certain that Job had broken faith with God. And they were tragically wrong.

Job knew that he had not broken faith with God. There was no secret rebellion that had stirred God's wrath (Job 31). Part of Job's pain was the physical affliction of being covered in boils from head to toe. Part of the pain was the grief of losing his children and, on a lesser level, his possessions. But the core of his pain was that he had no clue why this was happening, why God was not explaining it to him, or why God was allowing it to continue (Job 7:20–21, 9:21–24, 19:7–20). Job wanted an audience with God to air his complaint (Job 21:4–6, 23:1–17, 27:1–6, 30:20–23). Even in view of his extreme situation, Job's complaints before God are amazingly stout.

How did God respond to Job? We're amazed by what God did NOT do. He never explained Himself to Job. Scripture never tells us that God revealed the contents of Job 1–2 to Job—that Job's trials flowed from Satan's accusations and God's confidence in Job's faithfulness. God offered neither explanation nor apology. To the best of our knowledge, Job never knew the precursor that God has chosen to reveal to us. Is this because Job could not have understood it? Is it because Job made an errant assumption, that knowing the precursor, the reason behind his ordeal, would have helped him endure the trials? Is it because God chose to teach us about His absolute sovereignty? Such questions will be explored as long as this world stands.

How did God respond? After Job's many questions, God posed questions of His own. From Job 38 to 41, the Lord stunned, amazed, and educated Job with questions that document His holiness, power, majesty, and wondrous otherness. Job was moved to awe, humility, confession, and silence (Job 42:1–6). Come what may, he would not question God again.

How did God respond to Job's complaints? He gave Job a fuller understanding of His greatness. And in response to Job's trust and humility, He vindicated Job, restored his health, and blessed Job as never before.

## Moses

The burning bush stands as one of scripture's most memorable stories. God used the bush to get Moses's attention and used the conversation to call Moses to return to Egypt. Within that account, Moses's complaints against God amaze us. First came the excuses. "Who am I that I should go to Pharaoh and bring the children of Israel out of

Egypt?" (Exod 3:11) What if they ask about the God who sent me, "What is his name?" (Exod 3:13) "But behold, they will not believe me or listen to my voice ..." (Exod 4:1). "Oh, my Lord, I am not eloquent, either in the past or since you have spoken to your servant, but I am slow of speech and of tongue" (Exod 4:10). Finally came the attempted rejection, "Oh my Lord, please send someone else" (Exod 4:13).

God's response to Moses's rejection was threefold. God's anger was kindled. Are we wise to assume that Moses perceived God's anger, that Moses knew it was time to stop resisting? God met the concern expressed by Moses by adding Aaron to the team as his spokesman. Are we wise to assume that Moses knew God was helping him and extending a major kindness? We know that God did allow Moses's resistance to change His plan. As his complaint was rejected by God, Moses knew that he was going to Egypt to free God's people.

## Israel and the Exodus

The complaints lodged against God by the nation of Israel during the days of Moses are stunning in volume and intensity. Moses rightly anticipated resistance from the enslaved people he was sent to free. The initial meeting between Moses, Aaron, and Pharaoh led to the infamous order that the quota of bricks be maintained without the previous provision of straw. On some level, we grasp Pharaoh's logic: "If my slaves are so underemployed that they're asking to go into the desert to worship, I can give them more to do." The foremen of the enslaved workers first complained to their taskmasters, then to Pharaoh, and ultimately to Moses and Aaron: "The Lord look on you and judge, because you have made us stink in the sight of Pharaoh and his servants, and have put a sword in their hand to kill us" (Exod 5:21). It's a case of cascading complaints as Exodus 5:22 informs: "Then Moses turned to the Lord and said, 'O Lord, why have you done evil to this people? Why did you ever send me?'" The Lord showed remarkable restraint in allowing such stout speech. The core of His response was to reaffirm His plan to free His people.

Trapped between the Red Sea and Pharaoh's army, fear precipitated the next huge complaint.

> Is it because there are no graves in Egypt that you have taken us away to die in the wilderness? What have you done to us in bringing us out of Egypt? Is this not what we said to you in Egypt: "Leave us alone that we may serve the Egyptians"? (Exod 14:11–12)

While technically a complaint against Moses, in keeping with the teaching of both Exodus 16:8 and 1 Samuel 8:6–7, we treat it as ultimately a complaint against God. God's response was to have Moses reassure the people before providing a miraculous crossing of the sea and the utter destruction of Pharaoh's army.

After a short-lived celebration, the next complaints

dealt with bitter water (Exod 15:22–25) and hunger. We note the biting nature of their words, "Would that we had died by the hand of the Lord in Egypt, when we sat by the meat pots and ate bread to the fill, but you have brought us out into this wilderness to kill this whole assembly with hunger" (Exod 16:3). Their speech includes an astounding attempt at revisionist history and the impugning of Moses's motives. And God still responded with grace.

Exodus 17 begins with another complaint about water. The people's complaint against Moses precipitates Moses's complaint to God: "What shall I do with this people? They are almost ready to stone me!" (Exod 17:4) Again, God delivered, but the text reminds us that "they tested the Lord" with their complaint (Exod 17:7). We still see grace, but also an increasing displeasure from God. Numbers 11:1 documents that displeasure as the people complained, "and when the Lord heard it, his anger was kindled, and the fire of the Lord burned among them and consumed the outlying parts of the camp." Numbers 11:31–35 recounts not only the Lord blessing the camp with quail but also punishing the camp with a plague due to their complaints and disobedience.

Numbers 12 records the unsettling racist complaint against Moses by his siblings, Aaron and Miriam. The Lord defended His chosen servant. Aaron was pardoned and Miriam was healed of the punishment of leprosy only because Moses interceded for them.

Numbers 14 clearly states God's growing displeasure with His complaining people. In response to "Why is the

Lord bringing us into this land to fall by the sword? Our wives and our little ones will become a prey. Would it not be better for us to go back to Egypt?" God offered to annihilate them and to raise up a new nation from Moses (Num 14:2–3, 11–12). Only Moses's intercession preserved their lives. Even Moses's intercession could not save them all. Numbers 14:26–38 is chilling. Because of their consistent and vile grumbling, God pronounced, "Your dead bodies shall fall in this wilderness." Even that warning did not stop the rebellion of Korah and the associated loss of life (Num 16).

## Complaints Within the Psalms

The Psalms contain numerous complaints and strong calls for judgment against those who oppose God and His people (Ps 3:7, 9:3–5 & 15–17, 10:15, 18:37–42, 109, 137). Psalm 3:2 quotes a common complaint that unbelievers leveled against the Lord: "There is no salvation for him [the righteous person] in God." More importantly for this discussion, sections of the Psalms sound like direct accusations or complaints against God for allowing evil or delaying deliverance. In context, however, that view proves errant. "Answer me when I call, O God of my righteousness" (Ps 4:1) is actually an appeal for grace to the righteous God who has given relief in the past. "Give ear to my words, O Lord; consider my groaning," (Ps 5:1) is a plea followed by confession of God as King. Psalm 5 is worshipful and confessional rather than demanding or accusatory.

"Why, O Lord, do you stand far away: Why do you hide yourself in times of trouble?" (Ps 10:1) At first reading, Psalm 10 sounds like a complaint against God for His "delay" in judging the wicked. It includes a strong appeal for God's immediate action (Ps 10:12–13). Thankfully, our understanding of the psalm is tempered by the strong expression of faith in 10:16–18. Similarly, the beginnings of Psalms 22, 102, and 142 could be heard as complaint, but in context, they lean far more toward appeal and confession of need.

Particularly in light of 2 Samuel 6:6–8, we dare not assert that David never disagreed with God's actions. Yet, even within their frequent raw emotion, the Psalms display impressive reverence toward God.

## Complaints Within the Prophets

Jeremiah 1:1–10 has been read as similar in tone to the excuses of Moses in Exodus 4. The singularity of the "complaint" raised by Jeremiah mitigates against such comparison. We don't know his age, but Jeremiah saw himself as a youth who either is not able or is not qualified to speak for God. When the Lord told him, "Do not say, 'I am a youth,'" (Jer 1:7) and offered reassurance, Jeremiah obediently moved forward into service. Jeremiah's "complaint" can be easily understood as an expression of humility rather than an attempt to reject God's commission.

Ezekiel 4 offers a stunningly unusual example of a "change of orders" request made by a prophet and honored by God. God commissioned Ezekiel to employ diverse and striking object lessons. Within chapter 4, he is to portray the city of Jerusalem on a clay tablet and lay siege before it. He is to lie on his left side before the image for 390 days, then on his right side for 40 days. God commanded him to cook his bread using human waste to further display God's abhorrence of sin and displeasure with His people. That command was so troubling to Ezekiel that he asked God for a reprieve (Ezek 4:14), and God allowed him to substitute cow waste. Ezekiel even offered God a reason for his request—he had always faithfully followed God's dietary laws. Though distasteful in the details, this account stands as yet another example of God's grace, of God granting a servant permission to serve within the confines of his conscience.

Jonah's complaint against God is initially more obvious in his behavior than in his words. When commissioned, "Arise, and go to Nineveh, that great city, and cry out against it," Jonah infamously boarded a boat in an attempt "to flee from the presence of the Lord" (Jonah 1:2–3). When the people of Nineveh believed Jonah's mission and repented, "God relented of the disaster that he said he would do to them, and he did not do it" (Jonah 3:10). And Jonah 4 begins with an amazing statement: "But it displeased Jonah exceedingly, and he was angry."

He was angry with God for being gracious, merciful, slow to anger, and abounding in love. He was so angry that he asked God to take his life. Even after such a stunning complaint, God chose to confront Jonah gently through the shade of a plant and its subsequent death. And the book of Jonah ends with no report that Jonah accepted God's message and repented. What a fearsome example of anger shutting down grace and shutting out God!

The book of Habakkuk begins with one of the most direct complaints in all of scripture.

> O Lord, how long shall I cry for help; and you will not hear? Or cry to you "Violence!" and you will not save? Why do you make me see iniquity; and why do you idly look at wrong? Destruction and violence are before me, strife and contentions arise. So the Lord is paralyzed, and justice never goes forth. For the wicked surround the righteous; so justice goes forth perverted (Hab 1:2–4).

In an amazing double-down, Habakkuk 1:12–17 contains another striking complaint.

Habakkuk's complaints stand as an amazing example of God's humility, communication skill, and love for the righteous. The Lord had his prophet ask THE question of the day in the bluntest possible manner, so that God could address that question with wisdom, clarity, and perspective. The wheels of justice were already in motion (Hab 1:5–11). He even named the instrument of His coming judgment.

In response to the second complaint, God gave two of the greatest statements in all of scripture. "The righteous shall live by his faith" and there is coming a day when "... the earth will be filled with the knowledge of the glory of the Lord as the waters cover the sea" (Hab 2:4, 14). No wonder the entire final chapter is filled with a prayer of faith and a psalm of joy! God knew what was happening. God had plans in place that were not yet visible to His people. In grace, God exhorted His people to maintain trust and hold on to righteousness. God will always do right and save His own.

Outside the prophetic books, but dealing with a prophet of God, 1 Kings 19 offers an example of a similar complaint. After the utter victory at Mount Carmel, Jezebel ordered Elijah to be killed. Elijah fled in fear and asked the Lord to take his life. When asked why he wanted to die, the prophet stated his complaint:

> I have been very jealous for the Lord, the God of hosts. For the people of Israel have forsaken your covenant, thrown down your altars, and killed your prophets with the sword, and I, even I only, am left, and they seek my life, to take it away (1 Kgs 19:10).

How did the Lord respond to Elijah's complaint? Even before the grievance was spoken, God had sent an angel with food and water (1 Kgs 19:6). God gave Elijah strength for the forty-day journey to Horeb (1 Kgs 19:8). And God engaged him in reflective conversation.

After the grievance was stated, God showed Elijah an amazing manifestation of His power (1 Kgs 19:11–13). Within that display of power is the sweet reminder that God is just as strong in "the sound of a low whisper" as in fire, earthquake, or rock-crushing wind. Then, God sent Elijah to anoint two kings, assured Elijah that righteous judgment was coming, reminded Elijah that there remained 7,000 additional faithful souls, and gave Elijah a coworker. On top of that, one of God's ultimate responses to Elijah was to take him from the earth in a chariot of fire (2 Kgs 2). In a favorite example of biblical ironies, the man who complained and prayed for God to take his life was never allowed to die!

## Conclusion

What do we learn from our survey of God's response to human complaints within the Old Testament? The following list in no way claims to exhaust the answers, but we find it both encouraging and sobering.

It is both errant and ineffective to complain to God that His standards are too high, His judgment is too stout, or His help is insufficient. We find no biblical example where God accepted or smiled on an excuse for sin. There is no hint of God excusing humans from our responsibility to make righteous choices. Old Testament examples stand in solidarity with the master's response to the complaint of the one-talent servant in Matthew 25:24–30.

The Lord never promises to give account of His

actions to humans. While the Lord has often graciously explained His actions and shared His plans with those who love Him, He owes us no explanation. Humility demands acknowledgement that much remains beyond our ability to comprehend.

As a loving Father, the Lord is sensitive to human weakness, pain, and fear. Many biblical accounts describe God as hearing complaints without reproach or offense. We take comfort in knowing that God understands our struggles and our hearts. He loves us with amazing ferocity. He protects us far more skillfully than we can comprehend—even protecting us from ourselves.

Complaints tend to beget complaints. Complaint cycles and/or cascades can take on a life of their own. They are like the winds generated by a forest fire causing that fire to intensify and spread.

While the Lord is gracious and gives abundant space for growth, He does not appreciate continual complaining. There are limits to God's patience with those who refuse to learn and grow. Complaining that descends to the level of rebellion or rejection will be judged. With strong support from Jude 16 and James 5:9, 1 Corinthians 10:9–11 speaks directly of Old Testament examples.

> We must not put Christ to the test, as some of them did and were destroyed by serpents, not grumble, as some of them did and were destroyed by the Destroyer. Now these things happened to them as an example, but they

were written down for our instruction, on whom the end of the ages has come.

In the further words of Paul,

Do all things without grumbling or disputing that you may be blameless and innocent, children of God without blemish in the midst of a crooked and twisted generation, among whom you shine as lights in the world, holding fast to the word of life ... (Phil 2:14–16a).

Despite the Lord's amazing grace and patience, complaining against Him remains a dangerous choice. Questions are far wiser than complaints, and faithful obedience is wiser still—even when we do not get the answers that we seek.

## Note

This chapter first appeared as "God's Responses to Human Complaints," Pages 46–61 in *Things Most Surely Believed: A Festschrift in Honor of Charlie Wayne Kilpatrick*. Heritage Legacy Series. Editors of Heritage Christian University Press. Florence, AL: Heritage Christian University Press, 2021.

# Chapter 6

## *Prophecies of the Birth of Christ*

W hat a strange way to start a prophecy of Christ's birth! In the days of King Ahaz, the kings of Israel and Syria attacked Judah. While the enemy did not prevail, fear grew in the hearts of Ahaz and his people. Through Isaiah, God told Ahaz that his enemies would not prevail. In fact Israel itself would cease to be a nation.

To solidify Ahaz's confidence, God instructed Ahaz to ask for a sign. Ahaz refused this godly instruction (Isa 7:12). The Lord chose to overcome this obstacle by providing a sign for the king. Isaiah 7:14–17 details that sign. A young woman, who at the time of this prophecy was a virgin, would conceive and bear a son. Before that child reached the age of maturity, both of the kings feared by Ahaz would be eliminated. Matthew 1:22–23 tells us that Isaiah 7:14 does double duty in God's divine economy. Not only does that text make a promise to Ahaz, but it also predicts the miraculous birth of Jesus Christ.

Some scholars have made much of the fact that the Hebrew word *almah*, rather than *bethulah*, is used in Isaiah 7:14. They suggest that *almah* can refer to a young woman of marriageable age who may or may not be a virgin, and some conclude that it is improper to view Isaiah 7:14 as a prophecy of the virgin birth. The uses of *almah* in the Old Testament certainly include clear implications of virginity. The following verses cover all biblical appearances of *almah*: Genesis 24:43, Exodus 2:8, Psalm 68:25, Proverbs 30:19, Song of Solomon 1:3, and Isaiah 7:14.

How can we know that *almah*, as used in Isaiah 7:14, means "virgin" when it refers to the mother of Jesus Christ? Three facts lead to absolute certainty:

1. "Now the birth of Jesus Christ took place in this way. When his mother Mary had been betrothed to Joseph, before they came together she was found to be with child from the Holy Spirit" (Matt 1:18).
2. Matthew 1:23 uses the Greek word *parthenos*, which clearly means "virgin."
3. Upon hearing the birth announcement from the angel Gabriel, Mary's response was, "How will this be, since I am a virgin?" (Luke 1:34)

Though there would be no weakness if it did, the doctrine of the virgin birth of Christ clearly does not hinge on the definition of a single word.

As Matthew begins his narrative of the birth of Jesus, he writes,

> All this took place to fulfill what the Lord had spoken by the prophet: "Behold the virgin shall conceive and bear a son, and they shall call his name Immanuel" (which means, God with us) (Matt 1:22–23).

Matthew grounds his words in ancient truth. In doing so, he affirms that Isaiah 7 is Messianic prophecy. He also implicitly argues that understanding such prophecies should build faith in the hearts of God's people.

Isaiah 9:6–7 appears as beautiful, hope-filled calm in a sea of pain and distress. The Child, the Son, is a gift. Immediately, our minds go to John 3:16. Of the wondrous names listed in this text, how could "Mighty God" and "Everlasting Father" fit anyone but Jesus Christ? What other son of David has established a never-ending, ever-increasing kingdom of judgment, justice, and peace? And the fact that "the government will be upon His shoulder" begins with His mother traveling by imperial edict during her last month of pregnancy, extends to the flight to Egypt to escape Herod's plot, includes ongoing opposition by the Jewish rulers during His public ministry, and culminates in the cross itself.

Micah 5:2 documents that "the One to be Ruler in Israel" will come from little Bethlehem of Judah. These words stand as a tremendous example of the power of prophecy. From these words, chief priests and scribes were able to tell Herod where the wise men would find the Christ Child (Matthew 2:1–6). Though some mistakenly thought that Jesus was born in Nazareth of Galilee, they knew to ask the right question, "Has not the Scripture said that the Christ comes from the offspring of David, and from the village of Bethlehem, where David was?" (John 7:40–42). The seed of David came from the city of David, just as God foretold (Luke 1:8–20).

## What Shall We Learn?

God always knows all things: past, present, and future. He knew that this world would need a Savior. He knew that we would need every reason and encouragement to believe in the Savior when He came. The predictions of Christ's birth from the Old Testament demonstrate God's wisdom and love. Truly, "for whatever was written in former days was written for our instruction, that we through endurance and through the encouragement of the Scriptures might have hope" (Rom 15:4).

Surely God knew that some would choose to attack the unity, validity, and inspiration of the Bible. The prophecies of Isaiah 7 and 9 and Micah 5 linked with the birth narratives of Matthew 1–2 and Luke 1–2 stand as powerful evidence that "all Scripture is breathed out by God" (2 Tim 3:16). These prophecies also countermand the claim that Jesus was a good man who chose to "assume" the identity of the Christ. No one can choose the timing and place of his birth. No one can choose his lineage.

While the Jews of Jesus's day knew from Scripture to be looking for the Christ, still "He came to his own, and his own people did not receive him" (John 1:11). The majority of His own people failed to recognize their Creator and Savior. Even their accurate knowledge of Scripture did not bless them. Their knowledge did not lead to faith because it was not combined with genuine humility and willing hearts.

## Applications from Our Lesson

Just as Matthew expected his first readers to have full confidence in the prophecy of Isaiah, God expects us to have full confidence in every word of Scripture. Without the help of Matthew 1:22–23, we would never know that Isaiah 7:14 predicts the virgin birth of Christ. With that help, we believe without doubt. What God connects, we connect. And we love Him for helping us make those faith-building connections.

For our increasingly secular and skeptical world, the virgin birth presents a major challenge. It is logically and physically impossible. Either it is miraculous, or it is untrue. Many now view this doctrine as an impediment to faith. In truth, the virgin birth as prophesied by Isaiah and announced by Matthew is an impediment to faith on our (man's) terms. It demands that we first believe that God is God—all-powerful, full of wonder, and not at all bound by human limitations. If God is God, no miracle is difficult to believe. If He is not, then no miracle is possible.

We recognize Isaiah 9:6–7 as Messianic prophecy because of the many points of contact between those verses and the life of Jesus as described in the Gospels. In doing so, we affirm our faith that ultimately the Bible has but one author. Humans held the instruments of writing, but every word belongs to God.

As New Testament writers quote Old Testament prophets, they remind us that there is but one timeless God. God has loved us and planned our salvation from the beginning. Jesus Christ shines as the central message of Scripture. He stands as the ultimate proof of God's love. We love Him first, most, and always. We share His good news with all the joy that fills our hearts.

## Discussion Questions

1. Why would God include a prediction of the birth of Jesus in a sign being given to King Ahaz?
2. Why would God choose to include so many details in His foretelling of the birth of Jesus?
3. Of all the details of the birth of Jesus that are given in the Old Testament, which is most impressive to you? Why?
4. The devil has managed to use the virgin birth as a barrier to faith for some people. What

does this tell you about the devil? What does it tell you about human nature?

## Activity Suggestions

1. To prepare for this lesson: Read Isaiah 7:1–17 and 9:6–7, Matthew 1–2, and Luke 1–2. Read with this question in mind: How is God working to strengthen my faith?

2. To put the lesson into action: Identify the point from this lesson that most impresses you. Share that truth with at least two friends. Suggested conversation starter: "I was reminded of the most wonderful thing in my Bible class this week ..."

## Note

This chapter first appeared as "Prophecies of His Birth." Pages 41–45 in *Power Points for New Life*. Adult Bible Quarterly. Nashville: 21st Century Christian, Fall 2005.

# Chapter 7

## *Prophecies of the Death of Christ*

I saiah 53 speaks with such clarity—as surely as the Messiah must come, the Messiah must die. "He was despised and rejected by men, a man of sorrows and acquainted with grief" (Isa 53:3). "He was pierced for our transgressions; he was crushed for our iniquities" (Isa 53:5). "He was oppressed, and he was afflicted" (Isa 53:7). "And the Lord has laid on him the iniquity of us all" (Isaiah 53:6). And, according to God's eternal plan, He died for us.

"He was cut off out of the land of the living" (Isa 53:8). "He poured out his soul to death" (Isa 53:12). Isaiah 53 leaves no room for the cross as an accident or an afterthought. More than 700 years before Calvary, God put these prophecies into print. Isaiah 53:9 reads, "And they made his grave with the wicked and with a rich man in his death." Matthew 27:38 reminds us that He was crucified between two robbers—the wicked. Matthew 27:57–60 describes Joseph as "a rich man of Arimathea ... who was also a disciple of Jesus" who requested and buried the body of Jesus. Such details could only be known by God.

Even earlier, words that Jesus would speak from the cross were recorded by David (Ps 22:1). John 19:24 and 28 directly connect Psalm 22:18 and 15, respectively, to actions surrounding Jesus at His death. In both verses John uses notably similar phrasing: "This was to fulfill the Scripture" and "to fulfill the Scripture." As he connects Zechariah 12:10 and 13:9 to the actions of those who killed Jesus, John states God's purpose: "that the Scripture might be fulfilled" (John 19:36).

Zechariah 11:12–13 foreshadows the price to be paid for the betrayal of Jesus. Even more remarkably, Jeremiah 32:6–9 tells just what would be done with those thirty pieces of silver (Matt 27:1–10). And Matthew begins verse 9 by saying, "Then was fulfilled what had been spoken by the prophet Jeremiah ..."

## What Shall We Learn?

It would take amazing effort to miss the points of correlation between Isaiah 53 and the gospel accounts of Jesus's death. David, Jeremiah, and Zechariah bear the same detailed, consistent witness. Line upon line, these prophets prove that God's plan was set centuries before it unfolded.

As remarkable as these prophecies are, their predictions of the words and actions surrounding the cross are not the most astounding truth in these texts. What could be more outstanding than the prediction of specific details centuries before they happened? We offer two truths: the reasons for the cross and the accomplishments of the cross.

As noted above, Isaiah 53 unflinchingly documents the guilt of our sins. Jesus bore the full cost in His body. The sins of this world necessitated the cross. Your sins and mine cannot be taken lightly.

God did not wait for us to meet Him halfway. "For while we were still weak, at the right time Christ died for the ungodly" (Rom 5:6). "... God shows his love for us in that while we were still sinners, Christ died for us" (Rom 5:8). "... While we were enemies we were reconciled to God by the death of his son" (Rom 5:10). Ephesians 2:1–10 is even blunter:

> And you were dead in the trespasses and sins in which you once walked, following the course of this world, following the prince of the power of the air, the spirit that is now at work in the sons of disobedience—among whom we all once lived in the passions of our flesh, carrying out the desires of the body and the mind, and were by nature children of wrath, like the rest of mankind. But God, being rich in mercy, because of the great love with which he loved us, even when we were dead in our trespasses, made us alive together with Christ—by grace you have been saved—and raised us up with him and seated us

with him in the heavenly places in Christ Jesus, so that in the coming ages he might show the immeasurable riches of his grace in kindness toward us in Christ Jesus. For by grace you have been saved through faith. And this is not your own doing; it is the gift of God, not a result of works, so that no one may boast. For we are his workmanship, created in Christ Jesus for good works, which God prepared beforehand, that we should walk in them.

The accomplishments of the cross are amazing. "Surely he has borne our griefs and carried our sorrows" (Isa 53:4). "... With his wounds we are healed" (Isa 53:5). "Yet it was the will of the Lord to crush him; he has put him to grief ..." (Isa 53:10). The changes in verb tenses may be unusual, but we get the point. Jesus is our offering for sin.

Out of the anguish of his soul he shall see and be satisfied; by his knowledge shall the righteous one, my servant, make many to be accounted righteous, and he shall bear their iniquities. Therefore I will divide him a portion with the many, and he shall divide the spoil with the strong, because he poured out his soul to death and was numbered with the transgressors; yet he bore the sin of many, and makes intercession for the transgressors (Isa 53:11–12).

When we were God's enemies, He reached out to us with grace (Rom 5:10). He laid our griefs, our sorrows, our punishment, and our sin on the soul of His Son. As the just, holy, loving God, He paid the debt that we could never pay. And it was Jesus, "the founder and perfecter of our faith, who for the joy that was set before him endured the cross despising the shame" (Heb 12:2). We could never imagine a greater demonstration of righteousness and love!

While the physical tortures of the cross are implicit in the gospel accounts, those narratives are remarkably restrained. Notice Matthew 26:67–68 and 27:26. One explanation for that restraint is Isaiah 53. The Lord's suffering had already been documented in the most vivid and heart-rending of words.

## Applications from Our Lesson

As much as we prefer joy and peace, our lesson clearly teaches that suffering can be blessed and noble. Isaiah 53:2–3 suggests that one reason Jesus was "despised and rejected by men" is that He was "a man of sorrows and acquainted with grief." We know that Jesus did not meet many of the first-century expectations of the Messiah. Perhaps we need to be reminded that "It is better to go to the house of mourning than to the house of feasting" (Eccl 7:2). Struggles, particularly persecutions, can make us better people (Rom 5:1–5). If our Lord was not immune to persecution and suffering, we will not be either (John 16:1–3).

Further, we are reminded there are some lessons that can be learned only through suffering. Through the suffering of Christ for our sins, we learn so much about God's love and grace. We learn so much about the cost, power, and destructiveness of sin. Even Jesus learned from His sufferings, "although he was a son, he learned obedience through what he suffered" (Heb 5:8). He learned and mastered ultimate, selfless obedience. He experienced the ultimate human physical loss to fulfill His Father's will.

Isaiah 53 reminds us that even in times of great suffering, we can still make godly choices. In terms of behavior, "like a sheep before its shearers is silent, so he opened not his mouth" (Isa 53:7). Jesus's silence amazed Pilate (John 19:8–10). Peter gives us one reason that Jesus said so little during His trials. "For to this you have been called, because Christ also suffered for you, leaving you an example, that you might follow in his steps" (1 Pet 2:21). The very next verse quotes Isaiah 53:9. Even under the most extreme suffering, Jesus, "when he was reviled, he did not revile in return; when he suffered, he did not threaten; but committed himself to him who judges justly" (1 Pet 2:23).

Just as Isaiah prophesied, Jesus chose an attitude of trust. He left judgment and justice to the Father. He left vengeance just where it belonged (Rom 12:17–19). He did not allow the sins of others to provoke Him to sin. Jesus shows us that our responsibility to be righteous never wavers. He shows us that no matter what happens to us, we can choose trust, love, and obedience to God. Lest we think that this holy standard applies only to our Lord, Stephen's imitation of Christ is a shining example (Acts

7:57–60). God demands that we, too, be genuine disciples no matter what challenges we face.

## Discussion Questions

1. How is it possible for anyone who reads the Old Testament prophecies and the gospel accounts of the death of Jesus to doubt the inspiration of the Bible?

2. How does the vivid description of the suffering of Jesus in Isaiah 53 help us?

3. In light of the clear predictions of Isaiah 53 and Psalm 22, how are we to understand the prayer of Jesus in Matthew 26:36–46?

4. Does God literally expect us to show the same faith and grace in times of suffering that Jesus showed? Explain.

5. How can we come to view suffering as a blessing?

## Activity Suggestions

1. To prepare for this lesson: Read Isaiah 53, Psalm 22, Matthew 26–27, and John 18–19. Read with this question in mind: Why did God do all this for me?

2. To put the lesson into action: Based on what you have learned from Isaiah 53, pen a thank

you letter to God. Make the letter detailed and
personal. If you can, share your letter with
someone you love.

## Notes

This chapter first appeared as "Prophecies of His Death."
Pages 50–54 in *Power Points for New Life*. Adult Bible
Quarterly. Nashville: 21$^{st}$ Century Christian, Fall 2005.

# Chapter 8

## *God's Mystery Story*
### Ephesians 3:1–6

Most people love a good mystery, especially one with surprising plot twists and a super ending. No one knows us better than God, no one loves us more than God, and no one has filled our need for mystery at a higher level than God.

We love the mystery story of a childless man being called to an unknown country with the promise of becoming a great nation and blessing all humanity. We love the mystery story of a young man beloved by his father but hated by his brothers. He's sold as a slave, falsely accused, imprisoned, forgotten there for two years, and then "discovered" and elevated to indescribable power. We love the mystery story of a young man anointed king, loyally serving his king, being hounded by his faithless king, and eventually leading God's nation. We love the mystery story of a persecutor confronted by Jesus, taught the gospel, and commissioned as apostle to the Gentiles.

God has a long and storied history of revealing mysteries through His prophets (Amos 3:7, Dan 2:28). He delights in blessing His children with the knowledge that we need (Deut 29:29, Ps 25:12). For those who have ears to hear, God speaks (Ps 78:1–4, Matt 13:10–11). Powerful as these great stories are, they can't hold a candle to God's ultimate mystery story.

In Ephesians 2:11–22, Paul celebrates the unity of every believer in Christ. He extols the blood of Christ as THE POWER that has brought the Gentiles into the one body. Through Christ those who "once were far off have been brought near," given peace, reconciled to God, given "access in one Spirit to the Father," and "made members of the household of God." What a list of blessings!

As he writes these glorious words, Paul is a prisoner of Christ Jesus for them, for their good, for their salvation, and for their freedom from sin. Don't you love the play on words? Paul is literally a prisoner, incarcerated for the faith. More than that, he is a prisoner of Christ Jesus, a slave of Christ, willingly controlled and fully submissive to the Lord.

Paul is a marked man, a called man, and an empowered man. He views every asset and opportunity as manifestations of God's grace. What he knows of the mystery of God is to be freely shared. The knowledge was given to him for them! The Gentiles have a place in God's plan. They have a place in God's heart. The truth is hidden no longer! In God's perfect time, the Spirit revealed the mystery to His apostles and prophets. One God. One Lord. One gospel. One body. One inheritance. One promise. One way. Jew and Gentile are united in Christ.

Walls once viewed as permanent have vanished. People once viewed as aliens and enemies are brethren. Only God could do this. And it is wondrous!

Paul subtly reminds his readers of their debt to him. He is "a prisoner of Christ Jesus for you Gentiles ..." (Eph 3:1). While giving them every reason to hear him favorably, Paul is neither manipulative nor self-seeking. His status as "a prisoner of Christ Jesus" is part of "the stewardship of God's grace that was given to me for you" (Eph 3:2). This is way bigger than Paul or prison. God is at work, and everybody needs to know that.

All this was central to God's plan from "before the foundation of the world" (Eph 1:4). When the time was right, God acted to "unite all things in him [Christ] ..." (Eph 1:10). What a marvelous turn of events!

God's grace did not begin yesterday. God did not make this up as He went along. The best and brightest knew that something was afoot. Even the prophets and angels did not fully understand God's plan to save souls through Christ. The components of this plan were "things into which angels long to look" (1 Pet 1:12). Even the brightest of beings could not discern the mystery of God, the uniting of Jew and Gentile in Christ. Looking backward, the prophecies seem so clear. "And in you, *all the families of the earth* shall be blessed" (Gen 12:3).

It shall come to pass in the latter days that the mountain of the house of the Lord shall be established in the highest of the mountains, and shall be lifted up above the hills; and *all nations shall flow to it* (Isa 2:2).

"And it shall come to pass afterward, that I will pour out my Spirit on all flesh ..." (Joel 2:28). Only in retrospect do we understand. Only after God makes known the mystery can we see His holy hand.

When God redeems, He fully redeems! When God's mystery story is revealed, sanctified Gentiles are not given probationary status. They do not enter the kingdom as second-class citizens. From day one of gospel obedience, they are "fellow heirs, members of the same body, and partakers of the promise in Christ Jesus through the gospel" (Eph 3:6). Full membership. Full involvement. Full freedom. Full blessing and full responsibility. What God does, God does right!

## Transitions

God's ways have always been mysterious. Who but God would select one childless couple to begin His chosen nation or allow His own Son to be born in poverty and live infancy as a refugee? Who but God would let the denier preach on Pentecost or call the persecutor to preach? Who but God would allow His lead evangelist to work and write from prison? Part of God's ongoing mystery story is His amazing ability to use the most unlikely people in the most unlikely settings to accomplish His will. Prison bars may limit mobility, but they cannot limit service. They may limit freedom, but they cannot limit faith. God can work over, through, and around every circumstance.

When we walk by sight, we focus on obstacles and our limitations. When we walk by faith, we focus on possibilities and God's promises. Paul is honored to have been chosen by God for service. The call to God's service is always an honor, even when that is less than obvious. By serving faithfully, Paul opened his heart and his life to God's leading. By serving faithfully, Paul made himself increasingly available for God's mission. By serving faithfully, Paul was blessed to share in God's mystery story. That opportunity awaits all who step into the light of the gospel.

God's mystery story reminds us that God does not "do time." As an eternal being, God lives outside time. God does not regard time from a finite or mortal perspective. The greatest of all mysteries "was not made known to the sons of men in other generations ..." (Eph 3:5). The "fullness of time" had not come (Eph 1:10, Gal 4:4–5). The world was not ready. As with Jesus in John 16:12, God showed both patience and wisdom in waiting to reveal His mystery until hearers were ready.

The same principles apply in our daily walk with God. Even the Lord cannot tell us what we are unable to hear (John 16:12). Only Christians who "have their powers of discernment trained by constant practice" can be deemed mature and ready for "solid food" (Heb 5:14).

As we grow, God grants us greater wisdom and under-standing. As we listen to what the Spirit has revealed to the apostles and prophets, the Bible gives us under-standing of God's purpose and God's ways.

God's mystery story did not end with the revelations of Ephesians 3. Countless souls do not yet know God's love for them. They have not yet been invited to partake "of His promise in Christ Jesus through the gospel" (Eph 3:6). They do not know their place in God's mystery story. And some of them live in our town, on our street, or maybe even in our homes. We can tell these precious people the saving story of Jesus and His love. We can love them so that they will give us opportunity to speak. God's mystery story still moves hearts and saves souls. The gospel still unites people as fellow heirs in the same body.

What an opportunity! Everyone loves a mystery! During this week, find a way to share one aspect of the mysteries of God. Begin with a question, "Do you ever think about ...?" or a disclosure, "Lately, I've really been thinking about ..." Invite a friend to join you in contem-plating the mysteries of God.

## Two Caveats

While God reveals all that we need to know in order to love and serve Him, many spiritual mysteries remain. For example, we do not know the timing of the Lord's return (Matt 24:36), the exact nature of the resurrected body (1

Cor 15), the nature of Paul's thorn in the flesh, or what Jesus wrote in the sand (John 8:6).

The New Testament speaks of "the mystery of the faith" (1 Tim 3:9) and "the mystery of godliness" (1 Tim 3:16). Even these foundational aspects of God's truth remain a mystery to those who have not heard, believed, and obeyed. And in addition, some knowledge is revealed only as we participate in God's mission.

## Discussion Questions

1. Why did God allow His gospel plan to remain a mystery for such a long time?

2. What surprises or impresses you about the ways God chose to reveal His mystery story?

3. Why is it difficult for us to grasp the magnitude of God's inclusion of the Gentiles in the gospel and the promise of salvation?

4. What does the inclusion of the Gentiles in the gospel tell us about God?

5. In light of Genesis 12:3, Isaiah 2:2, and many other passages, how did the faithful fail to realize that the heart of God's mystery story is the unity of every believer in Christ?

6. Is it biblical to speak of our ongoing participation in God's mystery story? Explain.

## Activity Suggestions

1. How does our participation in God's ongoing mystery bless us?

2. As we think of "God's Mystery Story," what do you find mysterious about God's revelation and His dealings with humanity? List the mysteries of God that you still find wondrous. For each of them, explore the wonder. Why do they still intrigue you?

## Note

This chapter first appeared as "God's Mystery Story." In *Power Points for New Life*. Adult Bible Quarterly. Nashville: 21$^{st}$ Century Christian, 2008.

# Chapter 9

## *Jesus*

### "He Went About Doing Good"

We love Peter's famous description of Jesus to Cornelius and his family.

God anointed Jesus of Nazareth with the Holy Spirit and with power. He went about doing good and healing all who were oppressed by the devil, for God was with him (Acts 10:38).

We love Luke's attention to the actions of Jesus. "In the first book, O Theophilus, I have dealt with all that Jesus began to do and teach" (Acts 1:1).

We love the way Scripture urges every disciple to continue the "doing" that Jesus began. "Be steadfast, immovable, always abounding in the work of the Lord" (1 Cor 15:58). "Show yourself in all respects to be a model of good works" (Titus 2:7). Jesus "gave himself for us to redeem us from all lawlessness and to purify for himself his own possession who are zealous for good works" (Titus 2:14). Faithful leaders remind every Christian "to be ready for every good work" (Titus 3:1). "Those who have believed in God" are solemnly charged "to be careful to devote themselves to good works" (Titus 3:8). Paul urged Titus to "let our people learn to devote themselves to good works" (Titus 3:14). We dare not forget Colossians 3:17 and 23–24:

> And whatever you do, in word or deed, do everything in the name of the Lord Jesus, giving thanks to God the Father through him .... Whatever you do, work heartily, as for the Lord and not for men, knowing that from the Lord you will receive the inheritance as your reward. You are serving the Lord Christ.

As those who are committed to "do all in the name of the Lord," we're wise to look to the gospels—and beyond—and note the actions of Jesus as He lived in the flesh. If we do—as much as possible—as He did, we'll be poised to show Him the highest honor. And we'll be following the greatest of examples.

## Before His Public Ministry

Even before His public ministry began, Jesus set a powerful example of godly actions. Though he was God and was with God (John 1:1), He "did not count equality with God a thing to be grasped, but he emptied himself, by taking on the form of a servant, being born in the likeness of men" (Phil 2:5ff). What humility, what sacrifice, and what love!

We know amazingly little of the childhood of Jesus, but what we know is impressive. At age twelve at the temple in Jerusalem, "All who heard him were amazed at his understanding and his answers" (Luke 2:47). Understanding and answers speak of biblical knowledge and spiritual awareness; they turn our thoughts to Psalms 1 and 119. As his parents found Him after a three-day search, His explanation was, "Why were you looking for me? Did you not know that I must be in my Father's house?" (Luke 2:49).

We see the words of Luke 2:51 as summarizing His childhood both before and after the temple visit: "And he went down with them and came to Nazareth and was subject to them." Jesus showed lifelong respect for His mother (John 2:1–11, 19:25–27). At the same time, we love Jesus's steadfast refusal to put His physical family before God (Matt 12:47–50). We love the breadth and balance of Luke 2:52, "And Jesus increased in wisdom and in stature and in favor with God and man."

Shortly before His public work began, Jesus was baptized in the Jordan by John (Matt 3:13–17, Mark 1:1–11). Why would the sinless Son of God be baptized? "Let it be so for this is fitting to fulfill all righteousness" (Matt 3:15). He set a pattern of submission and obedience for us to follow.

Immediately after His baptism, "Jesus was led up by

the Spirit into the wilderness to be tempted by the devil" (Matt 4:1–11). Both weakened (physically) and strengthened (spiritually) by forty days of fasting, He defeated Satan at a level that made the devil withdraw "until an opportune time" (Luke 4:13).

Even as His public ministry began, Luke subtly reminds us of another of Jesus's regular practices: "And he came to Nazareth, where he had been brought up. And as was his custom, he went to the synagogue on the Sabbath day, and he stood up to read" (Luke 4:13). He didn't just attend; He was an active, contributing worshiper (Heb 10:24).

To summarize, even before His public ministry started, Jesus

- demonstrated humility, sacrifice, and love at the highest possible levels.
- prepared Himself for life and service through the ongoing learning of God's will.
- honored and obeyed His parents.
- grew in a well-ordered, balanced, God-honoring way.
- embraced a life of righteousness.
- followed the leading of God's Spirit.
- faced and defeated temptation through reliance on God's word.
- regularly participated in corporate worship.

# During His Public Ministry

Matthew 4:17 offers a key way to understand Jesus's public ministry: "From that time Jesus began to preach, saying, 'Repent for the kingdom of heaven is at hand.'" Luke 4:31–32 and Matthew 4:23 remind us not to make too much distinction between preaching and teaching. He proclaimed and explained; He warned and informed. In word and deed, He encouraged both repentance and godly living. Jesus called others to heightened levels of spiritual service (Matt 4:18–22, 10:1–32).

We do not possess the miraculous power of Jesus, but we love His example of helping and healing "every disease and every affliction" and welcoming people to bring "all the sick" to Him (Matt 4:23–25). We love the fact that He rejected both favoritism and financial exploitation. We love the way He praised the faith of those who trusted God (Matt 8:10–12, 9:22 & 29, 15:28). We love His practice of compassion (Matt 9:36). And we love His wisdom in limiting His actions when the people chose not to believe even in the face of mighty acts (Matt 13:53–58).

Jesus definitively corrected misunderstanding and misapplication of Scripture: "You have heard that it was said to those of old" (Matt 5:21, 27, 31, 33, 38, 43). He courageously opposed religious leaders who added to God's law and "shut the kingdom of heaven in people's faces" (Matt 23:13). How stunning! The scribes and Pharisees "shut the kingdom" while Jesus described Himself as "the door of the sheep" (John 10:7 & 9).

Jesus did not allow people to follow Him without first counting the cost of discipleship (Matt 8:18–22, 10:18–23; John 6:22–27). He welcomed followers—not on their terms—but on God's (Luke 9:23–26). He never tried to buy—or rent—followers. From the beginning of His work, He rejected shallow sensationalism (Matt 4:5–7). Though it must have broken His heart, He let people walk away when they chose to do so (Mark 10:17–22, John 6:66).

Jesus dealt effectively with critics. He did not let them control either His attitude or His actions (Matt 9:1–7). He didn't let potential criticism keep Him from calling Matthew, eating in Matthew's house, or preaching the good news to Matthew's fellow tax collectors (Matt 9:8–13). He even ate with a Pharisee (Luke 7:36–50). When appropriate, He answered criticism with Scripture and logic (Matt 12:22–37, 15:1–9), but He refused to perform signs on demand (Matt 12:38–45). And on other occasions, "He made no answer" (Luke 23:9, Matt 21:23–27). As needed, he raised the level of the question posed to Him (Matt 22:16–22). He quoted and explained Old Testament teaching, affirming creation (Matt 19:1–9) and the story of Jonah and the fish (Matt 12:38–41, 16:4). When proper, He bluntly exposed errant doctrine (Matt 22:23–33). He adapted His teaching—specifically through parables—so that true seekers could find, and scoffers would be left willfully blind (Matt 13:10–13).

Jesus practiced welcoming openness and transparency in ministry (John 18:19–21). He endured insult and indignity with grace (Luke 4:16–25, 1 Pet 2:21–24). He both urged and practiced interpersonal forgiveness (Matt 6:14–15 & 18:21–35, Luke 23:34 & 43). He affirmed God's forgiveness at a level far beyond the religious teachers of His day (John 8:1–11). He both taught and demonstrated that greatness in God's kingdom comes through service (Luke 9:46–48, John 13:1–11).

Jesus refused to be limited by social conventions when they would have limited His ability to do good and to teach the gospel:

- He healed a centurion's servant at a time when Roman soldiers occupied His homeland (Matt 8:1–13).
- He healed on the Sabbath (Mark 3:1–6).
- He touched a leper as part of the man's healing (Luke 5:13).
- He rejected unjust criticism of His disciples because it was based on human tradition (Mark 7:1–13).
- He valued the gifts of even the poorest people (Mark 12:41–44).
- He allowed a sinful woman to anoint Him (Luke 7:36–50). He treated her like she mattered.
- He allowed people who had been possessed by demons to follow Him and to give glory to God (Luke 8:1–3 & 38–39).
- He told the parable we know as "The Good Samaritan" (Luke 10:30–37).

- He talked with and accepted help from a Samaritan woman (John 4:1–42).
- He praised the faith of a thankful Samaritan (Luke 17:12–19).
- He called a rich chief tax collector "a son of Abraham" as He announced that salvation had come to Zacchaeus's house (Luke 19:1–10).
- He drove profiteering money changers out of the temple (Luke 19:45–48).
- He approved paying taxes to Caesar (Luke 29:20–26).
- He gave sinful people a second chance (John 8:1–12, 21:15–20).
- He washed feet like a slave or servant (John 13:1–20).

To summarize, during His public ministry, Jesus

- treated God's word as authoritative and worthy of respect.
- opposed the teaching of religious error.
- called people to repentance and righteousness.
- respected people's right to accept or reject His message.
- continually helped people with the goal of their salvation from sin.
- refused to let critics define or limit Him.
- urged and practiced amazing forgiveness.

- overcame social conventions that could have limited His work.

## After His Death and Resurrection

Just as the actions of the Son of God began before His birth as a human, they continued after His ascension from earth. We appreciate His encouraging words to the disciples who awaited the birth of the kingdom at Pentecost (Acts 2:1–9). At the time of God's choosing, the promise of the kingdom would be fulfilled. His disciples would bear witness of Him "even to the end of the earth" (Acts 1:7). God's words are in themselves actions; what God promises is as good as done (Heb 11:13, 2 Pet 3:1–9).

We both love and shudder at the scene recorded in Acts 7:54–60. In Stephen's final moments, he "saw the glory of God and Jesus standing at the right hand of God." It's repeated for emphasis. Whether standing out of concern, out of respect, in support, or some combination, we love what Jesus did for His courageous servant.

Jesus also appears in Acts 9, getting the attention and changing the world of Saul the persecutor. From his new understanding of blindness—both physical and spiritual— Saul was ready to be told "what you are to do" (Acts 9:6). Jesus prepared Saul, informed him of his future work, prepared Ananias to teach Saul, and washed Saul's sins away as he was baptized for remission of sin (Acts 2:38, 22:16). And we find ourselves commissioned for the same soul-saving purpose (Matt 28:18–20, Mark 16:15–16).

Acts 23:11 records another of Jesus's acts of love, comfort, and support. During one of Paul's darkest hours, he heard directly from the Lord: "Take courage, for as you have testified to the facts about me in Jerusalem, so you must testify also in Rome." In so few words, Paul learned so much. "I won't die immediately—God will deliver. By God's grace, I'll realize my longtime dream of preaching in Rome (Rom 1:8–13). My work for God is not yet done!"

We dare not forget the words of love, hope, warning, comfort, judgment, and correction delivered from Jesus to the seven churches of Asia (Rev 2–3). Jesus knew the trials and pressures faced by each church. He also knew both their actions and their motives. Their souls and service mattered to Him. Even as He graciously offered an additional measure of patience, He made clear that they were "on the clock." If they didn't act, He would. Jesus knows us just as well and holds us just as accountable.

We also delight in remembering that "Christ Jesus is he who died—more than that, who was raised—who is at the right hand of God, who indeed is interceding for us" (Rom 8:34). "He always lives to make intercession for [us]" (Heb 7:25). And He said of Himself, "I go to prepare a place for you. And if I go and prepare a place for you, I will come again and will take you to myself, that where I am you may be also" (John 14:2b–3). As He prepares for us, we're both wise and blessed to prepare for His return.

To summarize, Jesus continues to

- encourage His disciples through Scripture, through providence, and through the faithful support of other Christians.
- evangelize through those who follow in His steps (Luke 19:10).
- comfort those who struggle (2 Cor 1:3–4).
- expect His bride, His church, to love, to serve, and to be "holy and without blemish" (Eph 5:27).

## Responses to Jesus's Actions

Though Jesus did nothing but good and always honored God's will (John 8:27, 1 Pet 2:21–22), His actions met with wildly diverse reactions. During periods of His ministry, both individuals and multitudes followed Him enthusiastically (Matt 4:20 & 25). Ultimately, droves of disciples left Him (John 6:66). Even His closest followers fled (Matt 26:56). The crowd—that welcomed Him to Jerusalem as their king (Matt 21:1–11)—only a short time later shouted, "Away with him, away with him, crucify him" (John 19:15).

During a major period of His ministry, many people "heard him gladly" (Mark 12:37) and were "astonished at his teaching" (Matt 7:28). On multiple occasions, they marveled at His miracles (Matt 8:27, 9:8 & 33, 15:30–31). They even tried to make Him king by force (John 6:15). How ironic that John 6 also records their fickleness when they encountered more challenging truth (John 6:52 & 60).

Even during the periods of great popularity with the people, there were exceptions: "And behold, the whole city came out to meet Jesus, and when they saw him, they begged him to leave their region" (Matt 8:37). At one point, a village of Samaritans "did not receive him, because his face was set toward Jerusalem" (Luke 9:53).

During the bulk of His public ministry, the religious leaders opposed Jesus. "Some of the scribes said to themselves, 'This man is blaspheming'" (Matt 9:3). The Pharisees accused Him of working for and through Satan (Matt 9:34, 12:24). They questioned both His identity (Matt 11:1–3, 13:52–58) and His authority (Matt 21:23–27). On many occasions, they tried to trap Jesus with questions and hypothetical situations (Matt 15:1–2, 17:24, 19:1 & 7, 20:20–23, 22:15–18 & 23–32 & 34–36). They demanded signs from Him (Matt 12:38, 16:1). Ultimately, they plotted to kill Him and put both money and false witnesses behind their plot (Matt 11:14, 21:45–48, 26:14–15).

The responses of Jesus's disciples to His words and deeds were sometimes stellar. Think of Peter's confession (Matt 16:16) and the to-the-death loyalty of Thomas (John 11:16). On other occasions, the disciples stunningly disappointed Him. After his beautiful confession, Peter rebuked the Lord (Matt 16:22). Some of the disciples were indignant when Jesus wastefully—in their eyes—allowed a woman to anoint Him with "very costly fragrant oil" (Matt

26:6–13). Peter, at first, refused to let Jesus wash his feet (John 13:8). Peter bluntly denied a prophecy of Jesus (Matt 26:31–35). In the hour of His greatest need for prayer and support, the three disciples who were closest to Him fell asleep—three times (Matt 26:36–46). Even more amazingly, some of the disciples—and not just Thomas—had doubts even after seeing the resurrected Christ: "And when they saw him, they worshiped him, but some doubted" (Matt 28:17, John 20:27–30).

One question remains: What did God the Father do in response to Jesus's perfect life? He validated, vindicated, raised, and glorified His Son forever. Jesus knew this: "All authority in heaven and on earth has been given to me" (Matt 28:18). Peter made it the center of his Pentecost sermon: "Let all the house of Israel therefore know for certain that God has made him both Lord and Christ, this Jesus whom you crucified" (Acts 2:36). Paul states it beautifully:

> Therefore God has exalted him and bestowed on him the name that is above every name, so that at the name of Jesus every knee should bow, in heaven and on earth, and every tongue confess that Jesus Christ is Lord, to the glory of God the Father (Phil 2:9–11).

And John the apostle helps our understanding by lauding Jesus as "the faithful witness, the firstborn of the dead, and the ruler of kings on earth" (Rev 1:5).

## Conclusion

What an honor to be able, empowered, commanded, and blessed to walk in our Lord's steps. To be like Him, we must do as He did. "A disciple is not above his teacher, but everyone when he is fully trained will be like his teacher" (Luke 6:40). "A disciple is not above his teacher, nor a servant above his master. It is enough for the disciple to be like his teacher and the servant like his master" (Matt 10:24–25).

What a benefit and protection to know that even as we imitate our Lord, our actions will be met with mixed reviews. As in Acts 2, some will be cut to the heart and immediately seek salvation while others will mock. Though we can never be sure of human reactions, we can always be sure of God's perfectly stable goodness. It is wondrous, blessed, and more than enough to be like Jesus by doing as Jesus did.

## Note

"Jesus: He Went About Doing Good." In *Do All in His Name: A Festschrift for Mechelle Thompson*. Editors of Heritage Christian University Press. Florence, AL: Heritage Christian University Press, forthcoming (2024).

# Chapter 10

## *Connecting to God*

## Introduction

Youth and family ministers are often quite young—at least as they begin their official roles. Frequently, they're perceived as even greener than they are. They're stunningly wise to take 1 Timothy 4:12–5:2 to heart. Even 2,000 years ago, some older believers tended to question the wisdom, stability, and spirituality of young ministers. We know this trend didn't start in the New Testament era. Though God rejected his excuse, Jeremiah recognized that young people who speak for God often serve from a deficit of respect and gravitas (Jer 1:6).

Centuries before the church was born, Solomon (and others) authored an entire inspired book offering wisdom, blessing, instruction, protection, and understanding to the young man who would hear his father's instruction and "forsake not your mother's teaching" (Prov 1:1–9). He nailed the point emphasized in this chapter: Everything good starts and ends in connection to God. "The fear of the Lord is the beginning of knowledge" (Prov 1:7); "The fear of the Lord is the beginning of wisdom, and the knowledge of the Holy One is insight" (Prov 9:10). And the earlier we build a solid connection to God, the better (Eccl 12:1–7).

Paul addressed the matter beautifully with Timothy. Show the brethren your connection with and commitment to God. Don't give them a reason to doubt or question. "Set the believers an example in speech, in conduct, in love, in faith, in purity" (1 Tim 4:12). Give them reason to respect your work. And here's how you do that:

> Devote yourself to the public reading of Scripture, to exhortation, to teaching. Do not neglect the gift you have, which was given you by prophecy when the council of elders laid their hands on you. Practice these things, immerse yourself in them, so that all may see your progress. Keep a close watch on yourself and on the teaching. Persist in this, for by so doing you will save both yourself and your hearers (1 Tim 4:13–16).

God's help is essential to those lofty spiritual goals. Without a solid, dynamic, and growing relationship with God, what Paul commanded can't happen. The importance of a deep relationship with God is strongly implied by the emphasis on right relationships with older men, younger men, older women, younger women, widows, elders, and erring brethren. 1 Timothy 5–6 offers a clinic on right relationships. Paul couched his first letter to Timothy in the context of his grace-given right relationship with God (1 Tim 1:12–17). He strongly warned against the false ministries of who those who made shipwreck of their faith (1 Tim 1:18–20). He condemned those who tried to substitute the keeping of self-invented rules for a true connection to God (1 Tim 4:1–5). Only true godliness informs and enables true ministry (1 Tim 4:6–10).

Those who serve in youth and family ministry strategically embrace the sacred responsibility of helping parents bring up their children "in the discipline and instruction of the Lord" (Eph 6:4). We hold ourselves to the highest of human standards. We know God holds us to an even higher standard (Jas 3:1–2). We can't honor God's call without deep and abiding personal knowledge of the Lord. And no matter how well we currently know Him, the biblical call is ever upward (2 Pet 1:2–11, Phil 3:12–16, Eph 3:14–21).

All we assert below is predicated upon having obeyed the gospel and choosing to live in Christ (Gal 3:26–27, Rom 6:1–4, Matt 28:18–20). Without biblical faith in the redeeming blood of Jesus Christ, there can be no saving connection to God. Without being born again of water and the Spirit, we have no access to God's spiritual blessings (John 3, 2 Pet 1:1–4).

Essential 1: Assessment

Logically, we know that personal spiritual assessment makes sense. There are numerous spiritual inventories, both online and in print, but the following ten questions have served so well.

- To what degree am I currently connected to God (Gal 3:25–29, 1 John 1:5–2:2, Phil 2:5–8)?
- Am I "walking worthy" of God's call (Eph 4:1, Col 1:10, 1 Thess 2:12)?
- Do I live the reality of Matthew 5:3–12?
- Is the word of Christ dwelling in me richly (Col 3:16–17)?
- Do I practice love as described in 1 Corinthians 13:4–8?
- Am I putting to death the sins of the flesh and manifesting the fruit of the Spirit in ever-increasing measure (Gal 5:16–26)?
- Am I personally practicing 2 Corinthians 13:5?
- Am I consistently growing in the Christian virtues of 2 Peter 1?
- Is there any sense in which I'm claiming to know God but denying Him by my works—including my words (Titus 1:16)?

- Do I courageously and consistently help those
  around me ask and benefit from these
  questions?

Our most godly friends—and sometimes even our
critics—will help us stay real with these questions.

Paul offers an important caveat in 1 Corinthians 4:1–
5. Humble, measured, and biblical self-assessment stands
wise. But there's no wisdom in graceless self-condemna-
tion or in prideful pronouncements of self-righteousness.
God's guidance is key. God's word is the standard, but
godly mentors often help us stay real and balanced. None
of us are as bad as we think on our worst day or as good as
we think on our best. We want to practice ongoing assessment that's fair, paying strong attention to directionality.
God does so much to help those who are moving
toward Him.

## Essential 2: Biblical Understandings

If we think of connection with God under the heading
of "spirituality," much caution is in order. I collect defini-
tions of spirituality, both good and terrible. Until you have
read and carefully considered, it's very difficult to know
what any author means by "spirituality." The word is
frequently used differentially (sometimes even in contradictory manners) within a single publication. Usages/defi-
nitions range from the mystical and esoteric to checklists—

simplistic claims that if you manifest all these behaviors, then you're spiritual. Let the reader beware; much has been written that is not in step with divine revelation.

Below is the best we know to say about spirituality in terms of connection to God. It's the current edition of an outline that has been developed over several years as part of a graduate course on spiritual formation.

## DEFINING CHRISTIAN SPIRITUALITY

Christian spirituality is loving God with all our heart, soul, mind, and strength and showing that love by embodying the gospel of Jesus Christ (Matt 22:36–39, 2 Cor 5:17, Gal 2:20, Col 3).

Corollaries:

1. Those who are spiritual think as Jesus thought.

- Purposefully and joyfully seeking the mind of Christ (Phil 2:5–11, Rom12:1–2, 1 Cor 2:16, 1 Pet 4:1).
- Adopting the attitudes/mindset of Christ (Matt 5–7).
- Embracing Christ's understanding of the truth of God and the nature of reality (Eph 4:11–16, Matt 4:1–10 & 19:4–5 & 25:31–46).

2. Those who are spiritual teach as Jesus taught.

- Lovingly (Mark 10:21, John 8:1–12).
- Passionately (Matt 7:28–29 & 23:37–39).
- Consistently (Matt 5–8).
- Clearly (John 8:31–32, Mark 10:17–21).
- Faithfully (Matthew 5:17–20, John 7:16, 2 John 9).

3. Those who are spiritual live as Jesus lived.

- Walking as Jesus walked (1 John 2:6, Eph 5:1–2).
- Loving as Jesus loved (Mark 6:34, Luke 23:34, Eph 5:25, 1 John 3:16, 2 John 6).
- Suffering without retaliating as Jesus did (1 Pet 2:21–23, Phil 3:7–11).
- Growing as Jesus grew (Luke 2:52, Heb 5:8).
- Embracing the same purpose—honoring God the Father (John 8:29, Matt 26:39–42).
- Embracing the same mission—seeking and saving souls (Matt 20:27–28).
- Living up to the same holy and selfless ethics (Matt 5–8, John 9:4).
- Choosing the same life of service (John 13:1–14).
- Showing the same submission to God (Luke 2:51, Matt 26:39–42).
- Manifesting the same heart of sacrifice (John 10:14–18 & 15:12–14, 1 John 3:16).

- Showing the same love for the church (Matt
  16:13–19, Eph 5:22–32).
- Honoring the same commitment to prayer and
  worship (Mark 1:35, Luke 4:16 & 5:16).
- Showing the same concern for the outcast and
  powerless (Matt 19:3–15; Luke 4:16–19,
  5:27–32 & 7:36–50; John 4).
- Showing the same respect for marriage,
  parenting, and family (Matt 12:46–50 &
  19:1–9, Luke 2:51, John 2:1–12 & 19:25–27).
- Living the same trust in and respect for the
  word of God (Matt 4:1–17, 5:17–18, 19:16–
  22 & 23:1–3).

Essential 3: Practicing the Spiritual Disciplines

It's virtually impossible to lead others where we've
never been. It never works to call others to practice disciplines that we omit. The classic spiritual disciplines as
identified by Richard Foster (Foster, *Celebration of Discipline*, 2018) are prayer (Matt 6:9–13), meditation (Ps 1:2),
contemplation (Ps 78, 119:9–16), study (Luke 2:46–47),
fasting (Matt 6:16–18), simplicity (Matt 6:19–24, Luke
12:15), submission (1 Pet 2:13 & 18, 3:1, 5:5–7), service
(Matt 20:25–28), solitude (Matt 6:6, 14:23), confession
(Jas 5:16), guidance (Phil 2:1–4, 2 Tim 2:2), worship (John
4:23–24, Heb 10:24–25), and celebration (Phil 4:4). Each
discipline is broadly supported within Scripture; none
flows from a single verse or passage.

While we find Foster's book most helpful, we offer two caveats. While the practice of fasting is strongly assumed, it is never commanded in Scripture (Matt 6:16–18). However, finding ways to deny the flesh in service to spiritual growth is biblically mandated (1 John 2:15–17, 1 Cor 9:24–27).

Secondly, each of the disciplines comes in forms strongly supported by Scripture, but both unscriptural and ascriptural forms also exist. We strongly promote doing Bible things in Bible ways. Counterfeit versions—for example, meditation as emptying the mind to find answers from within or celebration that focuses on exalting self rather than edifying others and expressing thanks to God —would harm, rather than foster, connection to God. We're wise to identify and reject false versions. We're just as wise to avoid letting the prevalence of false practices scare us away from tools that can bless us.

Purposefully building stronger connection to God through practicing spiritual disciplines functions best under the following conditions:

- Always guided by Scripture
- Practiced within biblical balance—never taken to unbiblical extremes
- Practiced with pure motives—never to be praised by others or seeking to earn special status before God
- Practiced prayerfully

- Practiced with the support and accountability of faithful friends; think elders, senior ministers, fellow youth ministers, and parents of youth group members
- Practiced with joy and thanksgiving. All progress is from God
- Practiced with the appropriate balance of hiddenness and transparency
- Practiced with a continual commitment to using what we're learning to honor God and bless others

## For Further Study

I have taught a graduate course, Spiritual Development of the Minister, for several years. Below are select works that have helped that course. Please remember the fish/bones principle. The Bible is authoritative and God-breathed. Whatever accords with the Bible is fish; what doesn't is discarded as bones. Foster's books and the works by Dallas Willard have been particularly helpful. Steve Williams's "A Brief Guide to Devotional Reading" is outstanding.

Alerlund, Truls. "'To Live Lives Worthy of God': Leadership and Spiritual Formation in 1 Thessalonians 2:1–12." *Journal of Spiritual Formation and Soul Care.* 9.1 (2016): 18–34.

Chandler, Diane J. *Christian Spiritual Formation: An Integrated Approach for Personal and Relational Wholeness.* Downers Grove, IL: InterVarsity Press, 2014.

Chung, Michael. "A Pauline Definition of Spiritual Formation." *Studies in Spirituality* 27 (2017): 237–256.

Foster, Richard. *Freedom of Simplicity.* San Francisco: Harper and Row, 1981.

_____. *Life with God: Reading the Bible for Spiritual Formation.* New York: HarperOne, 2008.

_____. *The Celebration of Discipline: The Path to Spiritual Growth.* Special Anniversary ed. New York: HarperOne, 2018. (1st ed. 1978).

Gunnells, Timothy C. "Spiritual Formation: Process and Praxis." Pages 97–118 in *Living and Active Word: A Symposium by the Faculty of the Turner School of Theology Amridge University.* Fletcher, Daniel H., David Musgrave, and John Young, eds. Montgomery: Amridge University Press, 2020.

Guy, Cynthia. "Spiritual Disciplines: A Means Toward Christian Maturity." Pages 119–138 in *Living and Active Word: A Symposium by the Faculty of the Turner School of Theology Amridge University.* Fletcher, Daniel H., David Musgrave, and John Young, eds. Montgomery: Amridge University Press, 2020.

Hall, Elizabeth L. "Suffering in God's Presence: The Role of Lament in Transformation." *Journal of Spiritual Formation and Soul Care.* 9.2 (2016): 219–232.

Hindmarsh, D. Bruce. "Contours of Evangelical Spirituality." *Journal of Spiritual Formation and Soul Care.* 10.2 (2017): 195–206.

Howard, Evan B. "Contributions to Evangelical Spirituality." *Journal of Spiritual Formation and Soul Care.* 10.2 (2017): 237–247.

Macchia, Stephen A. *Broken and Whole: A Leader's Path to Spiritual Transformation.* Downers Grove, IL: InterVarsity Press, 2015.

McClendon, Adam. "Defining the Role of the Bible in Spirituality." *Journal of Spiritual Formation and Soul Care.* 5.2 (2012): 207–225.

Nouwen, Henri. *Making All Things New: An Invitation to the Spiritual Life.* San Francisco: Harper and Row, 1981.

_____. *Life in the Beloved.* New York: Crossroad, 1992.

Sheldrake, Philip F. *Spirituality: A Brief History.* 2nd ed. Malden, MA: Wiley-Blackwell: 2013.

Smith, Gordon T. "Inter-Generationality and Spiritual Formation in Christian Community." *Journal of Spiritual Formation and Soul Care.* 10.2 (2017): 182–193.

Stenschke, Christoph W. "Spiritual Formation and Leadership in Paul's Address to the Ephesian Elders (Acts 20:17–35)." *Southeastern Theological Review.* 5.1 (2014): 83–95.

Vanhoozer, Kevin J. "Putting on Christ: Spiritual Formation and the Drama of Discipleship." *Journal of Spiritual Formation and Soul Care.* 8.2 (2015): 147–171.

Willard, Dallas. *The Spirit of the Disciplines: Understanding How God Changes Lives.* New York: Harper and Row, 1988.

_____. *Renovation of the Heart: Putting on the Character of Christ.* Colorado Springs: NavPress, 2002.

Williams, Joel Steven. "A Brief Guide to Devotional Reading." Pages 175–186 in *Living and Active Word: A Symposium by the Faculty of the Turner School of Theology Amridge University.* Fletcher, Daniel H., David Musgrave, and John Young, eds. Montgomery: Amridge University Press, 2020.

## Discussion Questions

1. If a youth and family minister lacked a strong connection to God, how would you know? What would be the key indicators?

2. If a youth and family minister lacked a strong connection to God, how would that impair his ministry? What damage and deficiencies would you expect to see?

3. What are the advantages of a strong connection to God? What blessings, opportunities, and protections flow from strong trust in and reliance on the Almighty?

4. How might youth and family ministry best encourage youth and families to build strong connections to God? What would biblical intentionality look like attitudinally? Structurally? Relationally?

5. What are the major indicators that a youth and family minister—or ministry—is strongly connected to God?

## Note

"Connecting to God." In *Introduction to Youth and Family Ministry*. Edited by Kirk Brothers. Florence, AL: Heritage Christian University Press, forthcoming (2024).

# Chapter 11

## *Rules for Spiritual Formation*

The literature of spiritual formation frequently suggests that each of us create a Rule of Life, a succinct action-guiding biblical statement of spiritual direction, commitment, and practice. Try as I may, that doesn't work for me. What does work is creating Rules for Spiritual Formation. Perhaps it's that I need categories and lists. Maybe I need things to be bitesize.

As you engage this version of Rules for Spiritual Formation, please question it.

- Is the order sensible? What changes in order might help?
- What categories need to be added?
- Are any of the categories duplicative? Are any of them more accurately sub-categories?

- Are the cited passages applicable in context? Should any of the passages be replaced or augmented by other passages?

You know these questions assume that you'll read with your Bible in hand in a decidedly Berean manner (Acts 17:11).

I love lists, especially checklists. Rules for Spiritual Formation could never be a checklist, so they're written as prayers. Writing the rules as prayers helps my heart stay focused on God. Everything good flows from and through Him (Phil 2:12–13, Jas 1:17, Acts 17:28). He's the source of the knowledge, the creator of the opportunity, the source of the power, the motivation for trying, and the ultimate goal of spiritual formation.

Please don't reduce the prayers below to a checklist. Spiritual formation deserves better. Please don't read my prayer list as exhaustive. I'm actively seeking help in identifying gaps and opportunities for expansion. These "rules" express principles that foster spiritual growth. They're an invitation to heighten and deepen your journey toward Jesus. My desire is to be rubber-meets-road real. If treated as prayers—from the heart, "God I need Your help"—they will bless us. That's the reason for first-person language. When you read "I" or "me," don't think "Bill." Let the prayers be your own.

An appreciative confession is in order. For the Spring 2023 academic semester (when this was written), I was blessed to learn in surround sound on a daily basis. Each

Wednesday offered a one-hour spiritual formation class with 20+ undergraduates. Each Thursday featured a three-hour spiritual formation class with 20+ grad students. From class discussions, reaction papers, daily journal entries, reflection papers, book reviews, and plans for ongoing intentional spiritual growth, I was blessed to be immersed in the practice of spiritual formation. I loved the adventure. I loved the MAJOR help that God was providing.

## #1 The Rule of Opportunity

Lord, help me see the myriad opportunities for spiritual growth that You send each day. Help me to welcome those opportunities. Please keep me from closing my eyes or my heart (Luke 24:13–32, Acts 16:6–10 & 18:9–10, Rev 3:7). Don't let busyness blind me in the fog of life (Luke 10:38–42). Don't let me mislabel Your gifts as interruptions.

Lord, help me welcome each opportunity with prayer and serious thought. Help me to stay grounded in and guided by Scripture. Help me to keep an attitude of "I'll try" because it's an honor to serve You (Matt 5:16, Titus 2:7 & 14, 3:8 & 14). I'll try because servants need to try (Col 3:22–24). I'll try because I don't have a clue how You'll use any given opportunity to shake me up, wake me up, and draw me closer to Your heart.

## #2 The Rule of Service

Lord, help me better understand the heart of Jesus (Matt 20:25–28). Help me better see my need to be like Him (Matt 10:25, John 13:12–17, Phil 2:5–11). Lord, help me know that nothing's too good or too much for You (Luke 17:10). Help me be like Samuel (1 Sam 3:10) and Isaiah (Isa 6:8).

Lord, help me know that it's always an honor to do Your will. Help me want to abound in Your service (1 Cor 15:58, Gal 6:9–10). Help me remember that you redeemed and re-created us for good works (Eph 2:10, Titus 2:11–14).

## #3 The Rule of Obedience

Lord, please help me not to fall victim to my pride, selfishness, or illusion of wisdom (Prov 14:12 & 21:2). Help me know that even the best intentions count for nothing unless I act to Your glory (Prov 20:11, Matt 7:21–27, Jas 2:14–26). Help me to obey like Noah (Gen 6:22, 7:5) and Jesus (John 8:28). Help me to welcome the training that comes from obeying You (Luke 2: 51, Heb 5:8).

Lord, help me know that worship and sacrifice are meaningless—even insulting—without heartfelt obedience to Your commands (1 Sam 15:22–23, Isa 1:10–20). Help me know that You can't be my God unless Your word rules my life (Matt 7:21–23). Help me know that every act of obedience is a confession of Your power and grace (Phil 2:12–13).

## #4 The Rule of Assessment

Lord, you remind me in countless ways to consider my standing before You, my relationship with You. Help me examine and test myself by the standard of Your word (2 Cor 13:5, 11:28). Help me to continually consider my ways (Hag 1:5 & 7). Help me not to think too highly of myself (Rom 12:3). Help me never to think I'm standing when I'm falling or have fallen (1 Cor 10:12, Rev 3:14–22).

Lord, please protect me as I practice spiritual evaluation. Help me not to listen to "yes men" who'll just tell me what I want to hear. Help me value the counsel of godly people who will hold me to THE standard (Phil 2:5–11, Eph 4:11–16, Gal 4:16). Protect me from myself. Help me "judge with right judgment" and never apply standards to others that I don't first apply to myself (John 7:24, Matt 7:1–5). Help me not to be afraid to hold myself up to the mirror of Your word and to hold myself accountable. Help me not to let the devil make me forget Your grace or doubt Your love. Help me remember that not every spirit— thought, voice, teacher, book—that claims to be from You actually is (1 John 4:1). Help me be wise and honest without being self-deceived, arrogant, or paranoid. Bless me to remember how much You've blessed me so far and to relish Your ongoing help. Keep me from being comfortable with any sin. Keep me from getting spiritually lazy. Help me do my part to move toward You.

## #5 The Rule of Learning

Lord, guide my learning so that it isn't fruitless, vain, selfish, or destructive (2 Tim 3:1–7). Help all my learning to be in Your service and to Your glory. Help me remember that respecting You is the foundation for all knowledge and wisdom (Prov 1:7, 9:10). Help me learn to love Your law and trust its guidance (Ps 1:2, 119:9–16). Help me know that Your word will always lead me to Jesus (2 Tim 3:14–17). Help me to remember that even Jesus had to learn in the crucible of challenge (Heb 4:15, 5:8–9).

Lord, protect me from the illusion that I've learned it all or learned enough (Phil 3:12–16). Help me to want to know and want to grow (2 Pet 1:2–11). Help me to want to grow in grace, knowledge, wisdom, service, and love (Phil 1:9, 1 Thess 4:9–10, 2 Pet 3:18). Help me not to stagnate or slip away from You (Heb 5:12–14).

## # 6 The Rule of Forgiveness

Lord, I know vengeance belongs to You (Deut 32:35, Rom 12:19); help me not to presume and never to take what is Yours. Lord, help me to keep learning how much You love forgiveness and how good You are at it (Ps 103:11–13 & 136, John 3:16, Rom 5:6–11). Please help me to trust Your word and Your forgiveness more than I trust my own thinking or feelings (1 John 3:20).

Lord, I know I can't be forgiven unless I forgive (Matt 6:14–15, 18:21–35). Please help me to NEVER think there's an exception to that truth. Help me never to harbor hate or bitterness; it's too dangerous and too destructive. It dishonors You. Help me to know that Your act of love through Jesus is the standard for all forgiveness (Eph 4:32, Luke 23:34, Acts 7:60). Help me to be humble, loving, and proactive in forgiving others (Matt 5:23–24, 18:15–17). Help me not to offer any fake forgiveness that ignores or excuses sin. Help me stay honest and loving.

## #7 The Rule of Encouragement

Lord, please help me love everything that's good, blessed, and God-honoring. Help me be like Barnabas: a giver, an encourager, one who pulls others into Your work and closer to Your heart (Acts 4:34–37, 11:25–26, 15:36–41). Help me be like Jesus, choosing to notice and commend faith and good works (Matt 8:10–13, Luke 19:9–10 & 21:1–4, Rev 2:8–11).

Lord, help me cherish and imitate those who encourage me. Help me want to pay it forward. Lord, thank You for so many biblical examples of great encouragers—Jonathan, Ruth, Paul, Stephanas, and the whole Philippian church. Please help my encouragement never to be fluff, but to flow from faith and love.

# # 8 The Rule of Pain

Lord, help me to never waste a hurt. Help me to find Your blessing in every trial and struggle (Acts 8:4, Jas 1:2–5, Phil 1:12–18, Heb 12:1–11). Help me find a skill, an insight, or an attitude that I can use to help others (2 Cor 1:3–7). Lord, help me to get paid for enduring and walking with You. And thank You for knowing I'm not asking You for money.

Help me to never minimize or ignore the suffering of others (1 Cor 12:26–27, 2 Cor 11:28–29, Rom 12:15). Help me learn to pray more and deepen my trust in You. Help me to do what I know to do to bless others (Jas 4:17, 1 John 3:18 & 4:7–11). Especially in seasons of suffering, help me remember that You transcend the pain and use the hurt to build endurance, character, and hope (Rom 5:1–5). And I know You use suffering to make us long for heaven.

Please help me to keep a spiritual perspective on suffering. Help me know that suffering for and with Christ indicates Your approval (Phil 1:29–30). Your word describes such suffering as both honorable and blessed (1 Pet 3:14, 4:12–19). Help me take to heart that "the sufferings of this present time are not worth comparing with the glory that is to be revealed to us" (Rom 8:17). Help me not to be surprised by suffering—Your warnings are so clear (1 Pet 4:12–19, Matt 10:18–26, Jas 5:13).

Lord, may I never again choose to suffer alone, but to invite and welcome Your gracious presence and the help of Your people (1 Pet 5:5–7, Phil 4:10–20, 1 Cor 16:17–18). Help me not to hide my struggles from those who love me. Lord, help me not to bring foolish suffering on myself or those I love, whether through ignorance or sin (1 Pet 2:18–25). Help me to remember that sin always brings suffering. It opens floodgates that I can't close (Hos 8:7, Gal 6:7–8).

## #9 The Rule of Balance

Lord, help me not to be deceived with false notions of balance. Help me not to imagine that what You identify as sin is really okay if practiced in a measured way. Help me not to pretend that I can control sin. Help me remember the wages and the nature of sin (Rom 6, esp. 6:12–14 & 23).

Lord, help me remember that there are things I can enjoy in abundance with Your blessing (1 Thess 4:9–10, 2 Pet 1:2–11). Help me remember that there are activities that aren't sinful unless they get out of balance and come to control us (1 Cor 6:12–14 & 9:27). Help me remember that my body is not to be worshiped or valued above You (1 Tim 4:8, Heb 11:35–40, Rev 12:11). Help me remember the work/rest balance that Jesus demonstrated for our benefit (Matt 11:25–30, Mark 6:31, John 9:4). Help me avoid the extremes of laziness and drivenness.

Lord, help me find a better balance in my dealings with people. Help me avoid cynicism and tunnel vision (1 Kgs 19:4, 10, 14). Keep me from being deceived in pride or ignorance (Josh 9, Prov 14:15, 1 Kgs 13:18). Help me to know when and how much to trust others. Help me to know when and how much to trust myself (Prov 16:25 & 21:2, Jer 10:23–24 & 17:9).

# #10 The Rule of Joy

Lord, help me open my eyes and my heart to wholesome, beautiful, biblical joy. Your word affirms that there's an opportunity for joy in every situation. The joy of saving souls and serving You pulled Jesus toward the cross (Heb 12:2). The first Christians found joy in the honor of suffering for their faith (Acts 5:41). In Your providence, wisdom, and grace, there's joy in the formative power of trials (Jas 1:2–8). Help me embrace those stunning examples. Help me embrace Philippians 4:4 on an ever-higher level. I know in my head that there's unending joy in knowing You, serving You, loving You, and being loved by You. Lord, I need help knowing that in my heart (Gal 5:22).

Lord, help me love the small joys that You send—the sunsets, kind words, and sweet memories. Help me cherish the little gifts I receive and, even more, the gifts You let me give: seeing parents blessing their children, watching sweet old people love You and love one another.

Lord, help me never to leave a joy unshared (Rom 12:15). Help me see each joy as encouragement to share Your love and Your truth.

Lord, help me remember that You command and

expect joy. Help me know that my heart is wrong if it lacks joy. If I don't serve You with joy, I don't really know You (Deut 28:45–48).

## #11 The Rule of Thanksgiving

Lord, make me more grateful. Grateful for the air I breathe and the ground I stand on. I know it's Your air, Your ground, and Your grace (Acts 17:22–28)! Lord, help me to hate ingratitude—especially in myself (Luke 17:11–19, 2 Tim 3:1–2). Help me hate it enough to do better!

Lord, help me embrace Your command to "give thanks in all circumstances" (1 Thess 5:18). Multiply my faith and vision so I can see Your hand and Your heart even in the darkest times. Help me know that there's always a reason to seek, praise, and thank You. You're better to me than I can ever know.

Lord, help me see the connection between joy and thanksgiving (Ps 9:1–2, 1 Thess 5:16–18). Help me do just what Psalm 9:1 says, to "recount all of your wonderful deeds" so I can give thanks "with my whole heart."

## #12 The Rule of Humility

Lord, help me to be so impressed with You that I'm never impressed with myself (Rom 12:3, 1 Cor 10:12, Isa 6:1–7). Help me to see how distancing and distasteful pride is to You (Prov 6:16–19 & 16:5, Jas 4:6, Luke 18:9–14). Help me to hate pride more in myself than I ever hate it in others (Ps 101:5). Help me to know that pride kills—that it can kill me.

Lord, help me to see how welcoming humility is both to You and to others (Jas 4:10, 1 Pet 5:5–7). Help me to want to be humble; help me to pursue humility, so I can be like Jesus (Phil 2:5–11, Col 3:12, Matt 11:29). Help me to see the wisdom and power of His teaching on humility (Luke 14:7–14, John 13:1–17). Help me love, respect, and imitate those who walk humbly with You (Micah 6:8).

Lord, give me the heart and wisdom to know that love, service, forgiveness, obedience, and encouragement can't be valued or practiced without the foundation of humility (Phil 2:1–4). Help me know that I can't find Your kingdom if I live in pride (Matt 5:3, & 20:25–28, Mark 10:15). Lord, please protect me from myself.

## #13 The Rule of Love

Lord, help me to trust the answers Jesus gave about the greatest and second commandments (Matt 22:34–40). Help me trust His words from John 13:34–35:

> A new commandment I give to you, that you love one another: just as I have loved you, you also are to love one another. By this all people will know that you are my disciples, if you have love for one another.

Help me find joy, peace, security, and hope in the fact

that You are love and Jesus was the embodiment of Your love.

Lord, help me not to love things (1 John 2:15–17). Lord, help me not to love people in destructive and unworthy ways. Lord, help me not to love myself in selfish and sinful ways (Eph 5:28, Matt 22:39 with 2 Tim 3:1–5). Help me to love souls and to love sharing the gospel.

Lord, help me trust every biblical example of love. Help me embody Your description of love from 1 Corinthians 13. Lord, help me to love what You love: the church You created (Eph 5:21–32), truth (John 14:6), and the soul of every human—even Your enemies (Matt 5:43–48, John 3:16–17, Rom 5:6–8). Help me remember that love as You define it is never just emotion, nor is it without passion. Help me show your love to everyone I meet (1 John 4:7–5:5). Help me love You first, most, always, and better.

The path of spiritual formation is stunningly demanding, but it's even more rewarding. It connects us with the best people on earth. It invites God to draw us ever nearer. It makes us more like Jesus. And the adventure ends in the eternal presence of God.

# Chapter 12

## *God and Books*

A t first thought, we might assume that God has little use for books. Books help us remember, but God never forgets. Books educate, but God is all-knowing. Books take us to places that we could never go, but God is everywhere at once. Books relieve boredom, but we cannot imagine the sustainer of the universe ever being bored.

Surprisingly, the Bible tells us that God has high regard for books. Within this essay, please let "book" include clay tablets, scrolls, and books in the forms most common in our day.

God wanted the genealogy of Adam remembered, so Genesis 5:1 begins, "This is the book of the generations of Adam." It's important that people know their history and their ancestry. We aren't born into a cultural vacuum. Our roots matter. For better or for worse, our families help shape our lives.

Because of persistent rebellion, God planned to annihilate the Amalekites. Thus, the Lord said to Moses, "Write this as a memorial in a book and recite it in the ears of Joshua, that I will utterly blot out the memory of Amalek from under heaven." (Exod 17:14). It wasn't that God needed help to remember, but Moses, Joshua, and the chosen nation did. Perhaps the Amalekites did as well. If they knew these words of judgment, they should have been moved to seek repentance and life.

Moses knew that God keeps a book of the saved. Exodus 32:32 reads, "But now, if you will, forgive their sin —but if not, please blot me out of your book that you have written." God responded, "Whoever has sinned against me, I will blot him out of my book." God is particular about His book. It is His book. He includes, and He blots out. Though Moses's heart was clearly in the right, this was not Moses's decision. It's amazing to learn that God treats us better than we treat ourselves. He protects us from ourselves. He reminds us of both His grace and our limitations.

God used books—in the broader sense of written language—to meet diverse needs. When a husband accused his wife of infidelity, God instructed Moses to remember His written judgments on immorality. God said to Moses, "Then the priest shall write these curses in a book, and wash them off into the water of bitterness" (Num 5:23). The accused wife was instructed to drink the water. If she was innocent, the absence of consequences proved her innocence. If she was guilty, terrible things would happen, both proving her guilt and initiating her punishment.

Looking forward to the time when Israel would be ruled by a king, God had Moses write, "And when he sits on the throne of his kingdom, that he shall write for himself in a book a copy of this law, approved by the Levitical priests" (Deut 17:18). Not only was the king to commission his own personal copy of the Book of the Law, he was to "read it all the days of his life, that he might learn to fear the Lord his God by keeping all the words of this law and these statutes ..." (Deut 17:19). Doing so would protect him from pride and disobedience. It would even prolong the days of his kingdom.

Famously, God used the finding of the Book of the Law to initiate restoration in the time of Josiah (2 Chron 34–35). Hilkiah, the priest, found the book. He shared it with Shaphan the scribe. Shaphan took the book to the king. As they read the Book of the Law, they were convicted by its words. The king's humility and national repentance led to God's forgiveness and blessing.

The same kind of response was seen decades later in the time of Ezra and Nehemiah. Nehemiah 8:5 reads, "And Ezra opened the book in the sight of all the people, for he was above all the people, and as he opened it all the people stood." They worshiped humbly. Then, "... They read from the book, from the Law of God, clearly, and they gave the sense, so that the people understood the reading" (Neh 8:8). There were seven days of reading, followed by a sacred assembly on the eighth day.

Nehemiah 9 describes a second session of readings from the Book of the Law. After fasting and repentance, God's people read for one-fourth of the day. Then, they confessed and worshiped for another six hours. Not only did they read and worship, but they also put what they read into practice.

In Esther 6, the king tried to cure his insomnia by reading. His servants read to him from the book of the records of the chronicles. The reading reminded Ahasuerus of his unpaid debt to Mordecai. That reminder helped save the Jews from destruction.

We dare not claim that God had to save His chosen people in this specific way. But we recognize that God chose to use a book to protect and preserve His people.

After being tormented by his friends, Job spoke the words recorded in Job 19:23–26.

> Oh, that my words were written! Oh, that they were inscribed in a book! Oh that with an iron pen and lead they were engraved in the rock forever! For I know that my Redeemer lives, and at the last he will stand upon the earth. And after my skin has been thus destroyed, yet in my flesh I shall see God ...

We know what Job is saying. "I need a book. I need to know that my story will be told. I need to know that I'll be remembered, that I didn't go through this for nothing."

More than that, "I want people to know that I kept the faith, that my hope in God and confidence in salvation remained strong. No matter what happens to my flesh, God will raise and bless me!" What a noble description of the value of books!

In Philippians 4:3, Paul speaks of his true companions and fellow workers "whose names are in the book of life." In doing so, Paul is echoing Job 19. The truth of Job 19 and Philippians 4 is echoed in Revelation 3:5, 13:8, 17:8, and 20:12.

Some value being listed in *Who's Who*. Others appreciate being listed in publications of professional and philanthropic societies. Christians recognize that there is no greater honor than being included in the Lamb's Book of Life. Again, God doesn't need such a book to remember His own. Rather, God knows that we need the hope and encouragement that such a book provides!

Near the end of life, Paul wrote to Timothy from prison. 2 Timothy 4:13 records his practical requests: "When you come, bring the cloak that I left with Carpus at Troas, also the books, and above all the parchments." The apostle who met Jesus on the Damascus Road, who received verbal encouragement directly from Jesus, and who experienced visions of the highest heaven, still valued and needed books. He especially valued the old books. While we cannot prove the point, we strongly believe that Paul was requesting copies of God's Holy Word.

When Jesus chose to communicate with the seven churches of Asia, He used a book. Revelation 1:11 reads, "Write what you see in a book and send it to the seven churches ..." Because He used a book, we are blessed by

His words to this day. The Book of Revelation, challenging as it may be, assures us of the ultimate victory of Christ. Within that book, we read Revelation 20:12,

> And I saw the dead, great and small, standing before the throne, and books were opened. And another book was opened, which is the book of life. And the dead were judged by what was written in the books, according to what they had done.

God's books document our faithfulness or our rebellion. They demonstrate God's complete knowledge and flawless judgment.

God's example encourages us to value books. We recognize that books can be treasures on many levels. Sometimes their value flows from the truth that they teach. Sometimes their value flows from their ornate design and physical beauty. Sometimes we value books because of the special people who shared them with us. Always, we value books, especially the Book, as they draw us closer to God.

# Note

This chapter first appeared as "God and Books." *Gospel Advocate* 151.1 (2009):12–13.

# Chapter 13

---

## *How Does the Spirit Lead Christians Today?*

## Focus Passage

Galatians 5:25, "If we live by the Spirit, let us also keep in step with the Spirit."

## One Main Thing

The Holy Spirit leads, comforts, and strengthens all who walk in step with truth.

## Introduction

Galatians 5:16–26, Ephesians 4:17–24, and Colossians 3:1–17 clearly document that every Christian is in a spiritual war. Though we have been given life by grace through faith (Eph 2:1–10) and though we have been made children of God by faith when we put on Christ in baptism

(Gal 3:26–27), the war continues. The flesh intends to win, but God commands that we walk in, be led by, live by, and keep in step with the Spirit (Gal 5:16,18, 26).

While the paragraph above is true, the spiritual war didn't start with the coming of Jesus or the birth of His church. It began with the fall of Satan, continued in the fall of humanity, manifests through the course of Scripture, and will persist as long as this world stands. Without God's amazing assistance, it's a war that no person wins.

When Galatians 5:25 begins, "If we live by the Spirit," it is not presenting an option for disciples of Christ. "If" in this case means "since" or "because." It acknowledges spiritual reality. There is no other path to or manner of spiritual life. Romans 8 powerfully documents this truth. It is "the law of the Spirit of life" that sets Christians "free in Christ Jesus from the law of sin and death" (Rom 8:2). "To set the mind on the Spirit is life and peace" (Rom 8:6). Only "those who live according to the Spirit set their minds on the things of the Spirit" (Rom 8:7, Col 3:1–4). Only those who are "in the Spirit" and in whom the Spirit of God dwells belong to Him (Rom 8:9). The very Spirit who raised Jesus from the dead dwells in and gives life to the faithful followers of Jesus (Rom 8:11). "For all who are led by the Spirit of God are sons of God" (Rom 8:14). Romans 8:1–14 and Galatians 5:16–26 fit hand-in-glove in documenting the power and victory of life in the Spirit.

There may be many questions regarding how Christians are led by the Spirit, but there can be no doubt that we must be led by God's Spirit in order to please Him. There is no life apart from the Spirit.


## Going Deeper

Galatians 5:16–26 clearly describes polar opposites. We can walk in the Spirit and reject the desires of the flesh, or we can resist (quench, reject) the Spirit and live for this world. "The desires of the flesh war against the Spirit and the desires of the Spirit are against the flesh, for these are opposed to each other ..." (Gal 5:17). Scripture offers no option for comingling. Bluntly, those who embrace the works of the flesh "will not inherit the kingdom of God" (Gal 5:21). "And those who belong to Christ Jesus have crucified the flesh with its passions and desires" (Gal 5:24). There are but two options, and their outcomes stand in stark contrast.

Galatians 5:16–26 reflects the nuance, subtlety, and balance of spiritual reality. While "those who belong to Christ Jesus have crucified the flesh with its passions and desires," those desires and passions don't want to stay dead. They rear their ugly heads in the weakest of moments and in the darkest of manners. This truth is mirrored in Ephesians 4. (See also Col 3:1–17.) Though the Ephesian Christians were "saints ... faithful in Christ Jesus" (Eph 1:1), though they enjoyed "redemption through his [Christ's] blood" (Eph 1:7), and though they "were sealed with the promised Holy Spirit" (Eph 2:13), Paul still commanded them, "... You must no longer walk as the Gentiles do, in the futility of their minds" (Eph 4:17). He commanded them (and us) "to put off [to continually put off] your old self, which belongs to your former manner of life and is corrupt ..." (Eph 4:22). On the glowingly happy side of life, he also urged, "Be renewed in the spirit of your mind and put on the new self, created after the likeness of God in true righteousness and holiness" (Eph 4:24).

One biblical answer to "How does the Holy Spirit lead Christians today?" is that He leads us to align our lives with God's truth. He leads us to reject the values and behaviors of this world in favor of godliness (1 John 2:15–17, Col 1:5, Titus 2:11–12). He calls all Christians to "be all the more diligent to confirm your calling and election (2 Pet 1:10). He urges us "to walk in a manner worthy of the calling to which you have been called ..." (Eph 4:1). It's the Spirit-inspired word of God that urges us to "walk by the Spirit" (Gal 5:16), be "led by the Spirit" (Gal 5:18), and "keep in step with the Spirit" (Gal 5:26).

Another biblical response to "How does the Holy Spirit lead Christians today?" flows essentially from the paragraph above. Within the word of God, the Spirit identifies works of the flesh and the fruit of the Spirit. He identifies in lists of attitudes and behaviors, as well as offering examples through the stories of both faithful and unrighteous people (Consider Absalom, Balaam, Cain, David, Elijah, etc).

"How does the Holy Spirit lead Christians today?" He reminds us that God does not lead us without our consent and cooperation. Would Paul have written, "Walk by the Spirit," if we had no choice, no responsibility, or no role to play? Would he have commanded, "Keep in step with the Spirit," if it were not within our ability to do so?

"How does the Holy Spirit lead Christians today?" We think of Deuteronomy 6:1–9, Proverbs 1:8–9 and 22:6, Ephesians 6:1–4, and 2 Timothy 1:5 and 3:14–17. By creating, sustaining, and empowering families, God stacks the deck in favor of Christian character and faithful living. This principle of modeling and mentoring extends to those within our spiritual family (1 Cor 11:1 and 16:15–16, Phil 3:17, 2 Tim 1:13 and 3:10, Heb 13:7). The Holy Spirit strongly endorses the show-and-tell approach to growing in Christ.

"How does the Holy Spirit lead Christians today?" Surely God's providence and laws of cause and effect play a role. From the stories of Joseph and Esther, we see "ordinary" people lean into extraordinary opportunities to save entire nations. Our stories may never be as dramatic or impactful, but when we look back on times of growth, service, and deliverance, we know nothing to do except thank the Lord and give glory to His name.

## Application

A major application of the fact that God's Spirit still leads Christians today is to avoid foolish extremes. On one dangerous edge is denying that God offers any current aid to His children. On the other is asserting that the Holy

Spirit could never in any way lead a person to contradict the Spirit-inspired word. 1 John 4:1 remains exceedingly helpful: "Test the spirits to see whether they are from God, for many false prophets have gone out into the world." Testing demands an authoritative standard, and only the Bible fully qualifies.

Jesus's letters to the seven churches offer another strong application. To each church, He said, "He who has an ear, let him hear what the Spirit says to the churches" (Rev 2:7, 11, 17, 29 and 3:8, 13, 27). When God speaks, we need to listen as if our very souls were at stake!

A most happy application is to take heart from the fact that God's Spirit leads the faithful (Acts 5:32). Acts 9:31b describes the time of joy and peace for the church in the days after Saul's conversion: "And walking in the fear of the Lord and in the comfort of the Holy Spirit, it multiplied." Exploring the means through which the Spirit offers comfort to the church is a most worthy endeavor.

Of course, the most obvious application has been offered above. Follow the leading of the Spirit to root sin out of our lives. Embrace holiness and sanctification. "Do not gratify the desires of the flesh" (Gal 5:16). Keep crucifying "the flesh with its passions and desires" (Gal 5:24). Rather than giving in to sin, joyfully live in the Spirit by cultivating and celebrating the fruit of the Spirit.

## Conclusion

On this side of heaven, we may never know all the ways that the Spirit of grace leads, helps, blesses, and protects us. But we know more than enough to be eternally grateful. God has not left us to sink or swim without His loving aid.

We dare not move to autopilot, foolishly telling ourselves, "Since God's got this, there's nothing more for me to do." God gives us the marvelous blessing of allowing us to work with Him in the saving of souls—including our own (Phil 2:12). He challenges us to the lofty goal of seeking to be holy like Him. And He blesses every godly effort and victory.

## Discussion Questions

1. Do you think the prospect of being led by the Spirit frightens some Christians? Why might some find it scary or intimidating?
2. What are the dangers of overreacting to those who think God's Spirit leads Christians in ways or to degrees not taught within Scripture?
3. Why would any Christian resist or reject the leading of God's Spirit?

4. In what ways or through what means could a person resist the Spirit of God (Luke 7:30, Acts 6:10 and 7:51, 1 Thess 5:19)?

5. What is the relationship between our obedience and the leading of God's Spirit? Consider Acts 5:32 as you answer.

## Note

This chapter first appeared as "How Does the Holy Spirit Lead Christians Today?" Pages 7–13 in *Led By God's Spirit: A Practical Study of Galatians* 5:22–26. Berean Bible Study Series. Florence, AL: Heritage Christian University Press, 2023.

# Grace

# Chapter 14

## *Renewing Respect for Grace*

I 'm surprised that my file labeled "GRACE–MERCY" has not burst into flame! One article therein speaks of "those who have recently awakened from decades of trying to prove themselves to God and to man and of striving to earn a seat in heaven ..." In another, a brother laments the pain of hearing "another grace-only sermon." There's Leroy Brownlow's classic article, "Abused Grace—Rhapsody in Apostasy." Next to it is Jack Exum's stout statement, "The word 'grace' scares us, hushes us, puts us in a closet. 'Performance' is our word. We've been born to it, raised in it, and led to believe in our own performance and success. Grace makes us defensive ..." Further along, there's a classically balanced article by Cecil May, Jr., entitled "Glorious Abounding Grace, But No License to Sin." And still another article honestly begins, "When I think of God's grace and our understanding of it, I think of confusion."

According to some, the Lord's church has either severely neglected or utterly ignored grace until recently. According to others, "grace only" proponents continue their systematic, purposeful assault against faith, doctrine, and obedience. This much is clear: Extremes beget extremes. Even claims of extremes beget extremes. Sometimes our conversations about grace have been anything but gracious. Strawmen have been erected and torched. Strange claims have been asserted. My least favorite goes something like this: "I've been a church-going Christian for more than half a century, and until a few short years ago, I never heard a single sermon on grace." The counterclaim reads, "Now I fear that the Lord's church is in danger of being graced to death." How vital that we seek thoughtful, biblical balance in every doctrine and practice!

## Grace in the Old Testament

A crucial aspect of renewing respect for grace is renewing our commitment to hear the entire testimony of Scripture. Some have over-applied John 1:16–17: "And from his fullness we have all received, grace upon grace. For the law was given through Moses, but grace and truth came through Jesus Christ." Some have the mistaken notion that the Old Testament contains no grace. In reality, grace permeates both testaments.

We see grace in God creating a universe that He continually describes as "good." We see grace in God's treatment of Adam and Eve after their initial sin. God spoke with them, taught them, and even clothed them (Gen 4:21). He blessed them with children (Gen 4:1 & 25). The infamous "mark of Cain" was, in reality, a manifestation of God's grace (Gen 4:13–15).

In the days of the flood, humanity was preserved because "Noah found favor in the eyes of the Lord" (Gen 6:8). Abram experienced grace when he lied to Pharaoh (Gen 12:14–20), when he extended grace to Lot (Gen 13), and when he laughed at God's promise (Gen 17:15–22). He even secured a promise of grace for the gravely sinful cities on the plain (Gen 18), even though the terms of God's promise were never met.

Grace permeates the story of Joseph. Grace was the source of Joseph's every success (Gen 39:21–23; 41:16). God gave Joseph's brothers, especially Judah, space to grow and change. He gave Joseph time to heal and to understand how God's grace can transcend men's evil (Gen 50:20).

Grace permeates the exodus. In grace God saw the oppression of His people and heard their cries (Exod 3:7–8). In grace God gave His unwilling servant a helper in the deliverance (Exod 4:14–17). In grace God delivered His people, even as they feared and accused (Exod 14:10–14). In acts of grace, God fed, watered, and led them. In grace God gave them His commandments for their own good (Deut 10:13). In grace God allowed special provision for the poor (Lev 12:6–8), a provision that Mary utilized after the birth of Jesus (Luke 2:22–24).

Throughout the Old Testament, we are challenged by

the depth and persistence of God's grace. Though a generation died due to unbelief, God refused to abandon His chosen nation (Num 14:20–24). Though sin often exacted terrible costs, gracious deliverance was provided time and again (Num 16:46–50, 21:7–9, & 35:9–15). Through the period of the judges and the kings, acts of grace were frequent, impressive, and sometimes even shocking. Who but God would reach out to His people time and again as they repeated terrible cycles of apostasy, rebellion, and repentance? Who but God would put away the sins of adultery, deceit, and murder (2 Sam 12:13)? Who but God would send His own prophet to help David see his sin and choose to repent? Who but God would extend grace even to a man like Ahab (1 Kgs 21:17–29)?

No wonder the Psalms vibrantly extol the grace of God! God, by grace, makes the righteous man "like a tree planted by streams of water" (Ps 1). God, by grace, chooses to show mercy when wrath and anger are due (Ps 6:1–3). God, by grace, tells who can stand in His holy presence (Ps 15 & 24). God, by grace, shepherds His chosen (Ps 23). Surely, "The Lord is gracious and merciful, slow to anger and abounding in steadfast love. The Lord is good to all, and his mercy is over all that he has made" (Ps 145:8–9).

As majestic as it is, there is no claim that the Lord's grace is either automatic or deserved. Psalm 145:17–20 summarizes this truth in striking fashion. God is both righteous and gracious. He is "near to all who call upon him," as long as they "call upon him in truth." There is no claim that God will fulfill every desire of every person.

Rather, "He fulfills the desire of those who fear him…"
Verse 20 is clear: "The Lord preserves all who love him,
but all the wicked he will destroy." As vividly taught in 2
Samuel 12, God's grace makes no claim to erase every
consequence of sin. David was both saved and preserved,
but grace did not remove all the costs of his sin.

## Grace in the New Testament

Jesus Christ is the ultimate expression of God's truth and
God's grace (John 1:16–17 & 29, 3:11–21). The heart of
God is a heart of grace. There is no desire to condemn and
destroy. Rather, God marshals His every resource for
humanity's salvation.

Jesus embodied grace; "And the Word became flesh
and dwelt among us, and we have seen his glory, glory as
of the only Son from the Father, full of grace and truth"
(John 1:14). With stunning humility, He "emptied
himself, by taking the form of a servant, and being born in
the likeness of men. And being found in human form, he
humbled himself by becoming obedient to the point of
death, even death on a cross" (Phil 2:7–8). There can be
no clearer definition of grace.

Jesus lived grace. Of all the ways to heal a leper, He
chose a touch (Matt 8:1–3). Of all the people to compliment and help, he chose a centurion (Matt 8:5–13).
Whether demon-possessed, tax collector, infamous sinner,
or Pharisee, Jesus reached out to all with the gospel. When
criticized for His acts of grace, Jesus responded, "Those

who are well have no need of a physician, but those who
are sick. Go and learn what this means: 'I desire mercy not
sacrifice.' For I came not to call the righteous, but sinners
to repentance" (Matt 9:12–13). Even on the cross, He
extended grace to a man who had previously mocked Him
(Luke 23:39–43, with Mark 15:32). As if any more
evidence were needed, He prayed from the cross, "Father,
forgive them, for they know not what they do" (Luke
23:34). Even after the cross, He restored the denier and
allowed Peter a leading role in preaching the first sermon
under the new covenant (John 21; Acts 2).

The preaching of grace was not without controversy
even in the earliest years of the church. By inspiration,
Paul masterfully contrasted two proposed paths to salvation: justification by "works of the law" and justification by
grace (Rom 3–5). Paul leaves no doubt, "For we hold that
one is justified by faith apart from the works of the law"
(Rom 3:28). In one sense Paul's primary contrast in
Romans is between "the Law and the Prophets" (the
Mosaic Covenant) and "the law of faith" (the new
covenant). On another level, the Holy Spirit moved Paul
to masterfully contrast the principle of salvation by law-
keeping—those who do the deeds merit the reward—and
the principle of salvation by grace through faith—"the free
gift of God is eternal life in Christ Jesus our Lord" (Rom
6:23).

By inspiration, Paul knew how his words would be
misunderstood. Some would be tempted to say, "Paul,
through your emphasis on grace you have nullified God's

law!" His answer is definitive, "By no means!" (Rom 3:31). While there is no merit before God and even God's law cannot save, people need the knowledge of sin that the law provides (Rom 3:20). People need the consciousness of transgression that the law provides (Rom 4:14–15). Through Christ, "we have access into this grace in which we stand ..." (Rom 5:1–2). At the same time, "But thanks be to God that you who were once slaves of sin have become obedient from the heart to the standard of teaching to which you were committed" (Rom 6:17). Grace has never negated God's law. Grace has never negated the teaching of Scripture.

Of course, Paul was aware of yet another level of misunderstanding regarding his teaching on grace. Romans 6 begins, "What shall we say then? Shall we continue in sin that grace may abound?" Paul has just argued that the gift of God's grace through Jesus Christ is sufficient to save all who are united with Christ (Rom 5:15). No matter how much sin and offense might abound, "grace abounded much more" (Rom 5:20). Paul knew what the critics would say: "Your argument for the supremacy of grace has undermined the need for righteous conduct. You have used grace to give believers full license to sin."

Again, Paul's response is definitive: "By no means! How can we who are dead to sin still live in it?" (Rom 6:1–2). It is not that being baptized into Christ makes it impossible for one to sin. There is still a battle to be won (Rom 6:11–14). Rather, Paul emphasizes the fact that grace brings newness of life, grace crucifies the old man, and grace breaks the dominion of sin. The definitive response is repeated in Romans 6:15, "What then? Are we to sin because we are not under law but under grace? By no means!"

In our world of competing theologies, the imaginary conflict between grace and law continues. We most often see it couched in terms of faith versus works. Ephesians 2:8–9 is the lynchpin: "For by grace you have been saved through faith. And this is not your own doing; it is the gift of God, not a result of works, so that no one may boast." Ephesians 2:5 is clear in its assertion, "... by grace you have been saved."

Ephesians 2, like Romans 3–6, gives tremendous emphasis to the centrality of grace in salvation. Every aspect of salvation flows from grace. By grace God chooses to reveal Himself to us. By grace God gives us the capacity to understand His revelation. By grace we have the moral awareness to recognize our imperfection, to acknowledge our sin, and to see our "lostness." By grace we have been privileged to hear the faith-producing gospel (Rom 10:14–18). By grace, we like Timothy, have "been acquainted with the sacred writings, which are able to make you wise for salvation through faith in Christ Jesus" (2 Tim 3:15). It's by grace that we are able to stand in grace (Rom 5:2, 1 Pet 5:12) and walk in truth (2 John 4, 3 John 4).

Some have made a misleading error in how they speak of God's part and man's part in salvation. Some have spoken carelessly about these respective aspects of salvation to the point of implying that these "parts" are somewhat equal. Some have made the erroneous assertion, "When it comes to salvation, first you do your best, then God does the rest." Romans 5:6–11 clearly countermands this assertion. Ephesians 2 demands that we reject any statement that implies a diminished role for grace in the salvation of some. It demands that we reject any assertion that seems to imply that human effort is the major contributor to salvation.

Oppositely, others have wrongly asserted, "There is no such thing as man's role in salvation. Salvation is by grace alone; it is totally God's doing." Rather than being content with the language of Ephesians 2, they have offered what they believe to be a clarifying addition, either "by grace **alone** you have been saved" or "by grace **only** you have been saved." Such language negates the need for faith. It implies that no response is needed to God's offer of grace. It misses the fact that mere hearing of the gospel does not profit unless it is "united with faith in those who listened" (Heb 4:2).

Failing to read entire thought units is a cardinal error in Bible study. While Ephesians 2:8–9 stresses the fact that salvation cannot be earned by works, Ephesians 2:10 clarifies the relationship between works and grace. We are God's workmanship. We have been "created in Christ Jesus for good works." Good works are such a part of our identity in Christ that we are urged to "walk in them." Scripture does not view grace and works as opposites.

## The Multifaceted Nature of Grace

No passage presents the multifaceted nature of grace with more passion than Titus 2:11–14. We respect the grace of God because of its pervasiveness. In the person of Jesus Christ, through the myriad daily blessings of God, through the good deeds of Christians, and through Scripture, "for the grace of God has appeared, bringing salvation to all people ..." Rather than being private or hidden, it is both public and inviting. It is wondrously good news to be shared with the whole world (Matt 28:18–20, Mark 16:15–16). Respect for grace always includes diligent effort to spread the gospel.

Paul reminds us that God's grace includes an educational aspect. Grace teaches us. In that it teaches us, Titus 2:11–14 indicates that grace necessarily includes content —doctrine, truth. While grace rightly stirs strong emotion, there is more to biblical grace than our feelings. The New Testament clearly links grace and truth. 1 Timothy 2:3–4 reminds us that our gracious God "desires all men to be saved and to come to the knowledge of the truth." Certainly, as noted above, Jesus is the bodily manifestation of both grace and truth (John 1:17 & 14:6). Jesus Himself linked His teachings with salvation (John 8:31–32, 14:21–24, 17:17). Respect for grace always includes respect for truth.

God's grace includes a moral/ethical aspect, prohibiting certain behaviors and demanding others. Grace trains us "to renounce ungodliness and worldly passions, and to live self-controlled, upright, and godly lives in the present age" (Titus 2:12). Rather than removing or lowering moral standards, grace points us continually to the example of Jesus, who has both redeemed us "from every lawless deed" (Titus 2:14) and purified us for Himself. Respect for grace demands respect for the code of conduct commanded in Scripture. In direct linkage between the educational and moral aspects of grace, see Ephesians 4:20–24. Part of learning Christ and embracing the truth that is in Jesus is putting "on the new man which was created according to God, in true right-eousness and holiness." Part of having hope in Christ is purifying ourselves, cooperating with God in the process of sanctification, "as he is pure" (1 John 3:3). Grace, like truth, is not merely a doctrine to be believed or a gift to be received; it is a life to be lived (John 3:21). According to Titus 2:11–14, the grace-redeemed people show respect for grace through righteous living.

Grace includes a unifying aspect. The language of Titus 2:11–14 is communal. It emphasizes the unifying nature of grace as it purifies and creates "... his own posses-sion, zealous for good works." We acknowledge that grace also includes a personal aspect. The Bible never implies that someone can embrace grace on behalf of another. Ephesians 4:16 reminds us that the unity is enhanced as the body is "joined and held together by every joint with which it is equipped, when each part is working properly ...." Our personal growth is not self-serving. Our personal growth in the grace of God enables us to bless others. It equips us to be conduits of grace. Respect for grace must include walking "with all humility and gentleness, with patience, bearing with one another in love, eager to keep the unity of the Spirit in the bond of peace" (Eph 4:1–3).

God's grace includes a motivational aspect. We respect the fact that God's grace appears expectantly. As we respect God's grace, ungodliness and worldly lusts are going to be denied. As we respect God's grace, we live righteously, both anticipating and welcoming the glorious appearing of Jesus. As we respect God's grace, we reflect upon the sacrifice and the love of our Savior. We respect God's grace as we zealously embrace good works so that we may bring glory to our Father (Matt 5:14–16, 1 Pet 2:11–12).

## Conclusion

We dare not be scared or hushed by the wonderful, biblical subject of grace. The doctrine of grace should not make any Christian defensive. Rather than confusion or controversy, grace should make us think of joy—the joy of hope, the joy of salvation, and the joy of eternal, intimate relationship with our God.

Respect for grace is respect for God, for others, for Scripture, for truth, and for the Lord's church. Renewing respect for grace must begin with an accurate under-standing of the biblical doctrine of grace as embodied by Jesus Christ. It must manifest itself in a life of grace, the daily imitation of Jesus as we apply the truth of Scripture.

Renewing respect for grace is a daily enterprise, a daily opportunity, and a daily duty. It opens ever greater doors to service and blessing. It shows the world that we are the children of God.

## Note

"Renewing Respect for Grace." Pages 123–131 in *Renewing Respect: Rediscovering a Forgotten Virtue.* Nashville: Gospel Advocate, 2009.

# Chapter 15

## *Saved by Grace Through Faith*

## Focus Passage

E phesians 2:1–10

## One Main Thing

Salvation cannot be earned; it comes by grace through faith.

## Introduction

Romans 6:23 stands forever true: "For the wages of sin is death, but the free gift of God is eternal life in Christ Jesus our Lord." Ephesians 2:1–10 eloquently elaborates on that truth. Our problem with sin does not flow from any deficiency with God (Isa 59:1–3). Rather, it flows from His utter holiness and the inability of anything sinful to stand in His presence.

In that sin spiritually kills every sinner (Rom 3:23), each of us lies before God just as dead as the dry bones of Ezekiel 37. And we are powerless to raise ourselves. To be fair, our spiritual state is far worse than that. Not only has sin killed us spiritually, but it also rules and uses us as we live out our few remaining days (Rom 6:6–11).

But this is not the case for Christians! We **were dead**. We **once walked** in sin. We **formerly followed** the course of this world and the prince of the power of the air. We **once lived** among the sons of disobedience as children of wrath, but no more! God has acted through His beloved Son. What we most needed and could never even begin to do, God has done. And Ephesians 2:1–10 tells us how.

## Going Deeper

What are the options for salvation from sin? Several have been proposed. Ignoring Romans 3:13 and 1 John 1:10, some falsely claim never to have sinned. A modified version of this claim is "Sure, I've sinned, but never at the level that merits separation from God." What a sad misunderstanding of both God and sin!

Some propose that we can be saved by linking ourselves to the meritorious status of others—apostles, patriarchs, saints, or heroes. The Bible knows nothing of such linkage. It clearly asserts Jesus as "**the** way, and **the** truth, and **the** life" (John 14:6, 8:24; Acts 4:8–12).

Others propose to offset their sin by virtue of good works. On the scales of eternal justice, all that's needed is one more good deed than the accumulated weight of sin. That tips the scales to salvation and all is well. Paul will have none of that! From a legal perspective, dead people have no standing to act before God. Creatures have no standing to accrue merit before their Creator. Think of what Jesus said even of faithful servants: "So you also, when you have done all that you were commanded, say, 'We are unprofitable servants, we have only done what was our duty'" (Luke 17:10).

Knowing the frailty of the argument above, others offer a modification. "Yes, salvation is by grace through faith, but that's not the whole story. God lets us do all that we can toward our eternal salvation; then by grace through faith, He mercifully supplies what we lack." This sounds so good, especially in our individualistic Western culture. But it's stunningly opposite Ephesians 2:1–10. We don't supply. We can't supply. God raises us from spiritual death, saving us by grace through faith: "It is the gift of God, not a result of works." That in no sense opposes choosing to believe God and choosing to obey the gospel. Rather, it clearly and forcefully reminds us that works of merit have nothing to do with salvation from sin.

This section of Paul's letter beautifully describes God's motivation for saving us by grace through faith.

Ephesians 2:1–4 documents that God knew our hopeless state. He not only knew, He cared. He refused to leave us without recourse.

Our text extols God's virtues that led Him to send Jesus on our behalf. He is "rich in mercy." He has great love for us—how beautifully Ephesians 4:4 echoes Romans 5:6–8. He loves to unite: "He made us alive together with Christ" (Eph 4:5). He acts from, shows, and shares "the immeasurable riches of His grace" (Eph 4:7). He acts from astounding kindness (Eph 4:7). And He loves to create people capable of sharing in the good works of His dear Son (Eph 4:10).

We often speak of grace as unmerited favor. God's grace is both unmerited and unmeritable. Without the grace of His written revelation, we could know only what creation tells us (Ps 19, Rom 1:20). From His revelation, we learn so much more of His power, goodness, and character.

Biblically we speak of faith as "the assurance of things hoped for, the conviction of things not seen" (Heb 11:1). More broadly, faith is trusting, obeying, and embodying both the attitude and the doctrine of Christ. It never lacks passion, commitment, obligation, or purpose. It pulls us ever upward toward the mission and the heart of God.

How should we understand Ephesians 2:9, "not a result of works, so that no one may boast"? God is stunningly anti-pride because pride is stunningly anti-God. Human pride seeks to deny God's sovereign reign. On some level, human pride says, "I don't need God. I can handle life on my own." Ephesians 2:1–10 destroys that myth. The dead have no life, no power, no hope, and no recourse. Those who hold on to pride have no way to accept salvation by grace through faith. Such people will be saved on their terms or not at all. God offers no such option.

Ephesians 2:9 may also be preparatory. Those ruled by pride are not ready for life in the kingdom. They will chafe at God's commands, finding them burdensome (1 John 5:1–3). They will resist God's leading and deny themselves the joy of serving God fully out of love.

Scripture has a wonderful way of turning life right-side-up. That's part of the beauty of Ephesians 2:10. We don't work to earn or merit salvation. We're saved so that we can know the blessings of serving others to the glory of God. Titus 2:13–14 elaborates: "Our great God and Savior Jesus Christ ... gave himself for us to redeem us from all lawlessness and to purify for himself a people for his own possession who are zealous for good works." We are saved so we can become God's people of good works. It's a superb part of being a new creation in Christ (2 Cor 5:17). Only through Christ are we qualified to serve God (Heb 13:15–16). In Christ, good works help form the core of our identity.

## Application

What did Paul want the Ephesian Christians to do with the words of Ephesians 2:1–10? The remainder of the chapter offers three answers. We are to recognize, appreciate, and build upon our grace-created unity with all who are in Christ. We are to glorify God for His majestic gift of Jesus Christ. And we are to live up to our God-given standing as the living temple of God. We have so much to live up to. Ephesians 4:17–5:21 implores us to become what God has made us. As we continue "to grow up in every way into him who is the head" (Eph 4:15), we have boundless good news to share with others. Everyone must hear this message of hope!

From within the text itself, we are to marvel at what God has done for us. Spiritually speaking, He has raised us from the dead. He has made us alive together with Jesus. And "he has sealed us in the heavenly places in Christ Jesus." The more those truths fill our minds, the more amazement, gratitude, and joy will fill our hearts.

Knowing the woeful prevalence and depth of misunderstanding surrounding salvation by grace through faith and the relationship between faith and works, we speak God's truth clearly and in love. Salvation by merit is false and hopeless. "So also faith by itself, if it does not have works, is dead" (Jas 2:17). False teaching leads only to false hope.

Without doubt, Ephesians 2:1–10 calls on us to renounce and resist pride. We could not save ourselves, and we did not save ourselves. Only by grace through faith is there any hope. By grace through faith, hope abounds, anchors, and advances until it ends in glorious sight.

Finally, our text also moves us to be what we are: "his [God's] workmanship, created in Christ Jesus for good works." We give Him our best while asking Him to make our best better (Col 3:23–24, Matt 25:20–21 & 29).

## Conclusion

What a matchless God we serve! What we could not do, He did. What we most needed, He provided at the greatest of costs. He makes us both His workmanship and His workers—allowing us the dual honor of living for Him now and living with Him forever.

## Discussion Questions

1. Why does Ephesians 2:1–10 continue to stir such passionate debate among people who believe in Jesus Christ?
2. What are the spiritual dangers of thinking that we somehow earn our salvation?
3. What are the dangers of denying that Christians must be people of continual good works?
4. Why is it impossible to be saved by works of merit?

5. Make a list of good works that God has made available for you to both demonstrate and grow your faith.

## Note

"Saved by Grace Through Faith." Pages 16–22 in *For the Glory of God: Christ and the Church in Ephesians.* Berean Study Series. Florence, AL: Heritage Christian University Press, 2021.

# Chapter 16

## *The Darker the Sin ...*

## Focus Passage

"...the Lord knows how to rescue the godly from trials, and to keep the unrighteous under punishment until the day of judgment" (2 Pet 2:9).

## One Main Thing

God's grace is deeper, stronger, wider, and more surprising than we can imagine.

## Introduction

Abraham's relative Lot is not a man we associate with grace. Generally, we remember him for bad choices that had tragic consequences. He made the selfish decision to take the well-watered plain of Jordan when Abraham offered him his choice of grazing land (Gen 13:5–11). In one of the classic biblical examples of foreshadowing, "he pitched his tent even as far as Sodom" (Genesis 13:12). Eventually he chose to live in Sodom (Gen 14:12). This led to his kidnapping and need for rescue by Abraham and his servants (Gen 14:13–16). We understand why some view the kidnapping as a message to Lot that he was in the wrong place with the wrong people.

In a sense, Lot was rescued twice by his famous relative. As God informed Abraham of the coming destruction of the cities on the plain, Abraham interceded for those cities with the memorable question, "Would you also destroy the righteous with the wicked?" (Gen 18:22). Not even the Lord's minimum number of ten righteous people could be found. Still, God's angels warned Lot. Lot and two daughters were saved from the fire, but then comes one of the darkest episodes in all of Scripture (Gen 19:30–38). Two of the strongest enemies of ancient Israel originated from those sins. Yet, Lot ultimately stands as a stunning example of the surprising and persistent power of God's grace.

## Going Deeper

In Genesis we note several examples of God's favor toward Lot. The Lord blessed both Abraham and Lot materially. "... Their possessions were so great that they could not dwell together" (Gen 13:6). The Lord blessed

Lot with a magnanimous relative in Abraham (Gen 13:9–10). The Lord blessed Lot with safety within "exceedingly wicked" Sodom (Gen 13:13). The Lord blessed Lot with rescue of both his people and his property (Gen 14:16). The Lord blessed Lot and his wife with children, though we neither condone nor understand his proposed action toward those daughters in Genesis 19:8. Lot was blessed to be warned of the coming destruction of Sodom and to be urged out of the city (Gen 19:15–17). The text emphasizes that this was "the Lord being merciful to him." The Lord even granted Lot's request to escape to the city of Zoar, rather than fleeing directly to the mountains (Gen 19:17–22). Lot received grace after grace from God.

Between his dark episodes, Lot showed grace to others. He knew the danger that the two visitors to Sodom faced, so he "insisted strongly" that they enter the protection and hospitality of his house (Gen 19:1–3). He tried to protect them at personal risk (Gen 19:4–10). Lot cared for the lives of his sons-in-law, even to the point of lingering in Sodom to the cusp of the destruction (Gen 19:14–16).

While we appreciate biblical fairness and balance, the account of Lot in Genesis ends on a terrible note. If that were the end of the biblical account of Lot, we would never think of him as an example of God's grace.

The story of Lot resumes in 2 Peter 2, a chapter that stoutly announces God's certain judgment on false teachers and all who live in rebellion. But 2 Peter 2 also documents God's grace, His ability to save, and His record of saving the righteous from the worst of circumstances.

The evil world perished in the flood, but Noah, a preacher of righteousness, and seven others were saved (2 Pet 2:5). Sodom and Gomorrah were turned into ashes, but the Lord "rescued righteous Lot" (2 Pet 2:7). For emphasis, Lot is also described a "righteous man" with a "righteous soul" and one of "the godly" (2 Pet 2:8–9). Amazing!

The devil would love for us to misunderstand 2 Peter 2. He would love for us to ignore the whole of Scripture and conclude that Lot's sin never really mattered, that God arbitrarily closed His eyes (Isa 59:1–3, Rom 3:23 & 6:23). He would love for us to doubt the accuracy of Genesis or to view 2 Peter 2 as contradicting it. Short of that, he would love for us to declare the Bible beyond our understanding so that we would abandon its study.

How can 2 Peter 2:4–11 make sense in light of Lot's terrible actions recorded in Genesis? In a word, grace. God did not save Lot in his sin (Ezek 18:27–32). God saved Lot from his sin. Admittedly, the Genesis account does not document Lot's repentance. This stands as a great reminder of the brevity of Scripture. Numerous accounts don't end with the neat closure that we often prefer.

2 Peter 2 offers insight into the reasons Peter, by inspiration, could describe Lot as righteous. Lot was in Sodom, but he was not of Sodom (1 John 2:15–17). Lot did not stop recognizing sin as sin (2 Pet 2:7). Lot was tormented (troubled, grieved, afflicted) by the sins of those around him (2 Pet 2:8). And God delivered Lot from imminent destruction (2 Pet 2:9). In the end, Lot's complicated and often lamentable story documents the triumph of God's

grace in the life of a deeply flawed man. Lot's story is our story of the wondrous power of grace.

## Application

False applications are easy to list. "All's well that ends well. Despite all his sins, the biblical account of Lot ends on a positive note. His sins were really no big deal." Lot's bad choices put many good people in danger. Lot's sins cost him his wife, his sons-in-law, and his reputation. We have no clue how Lot's daughters could have ever looked him in the eye again. Without Lot's sins, would there have been any Ammonites or Moabites to afflict Israel throughout much of Old Testament history (Num 22–25; Judg 3, 10, 11; 2 Sam 12)? The story of Lot intersects Romans 6:1–2, "What shall we say then? Are we to continue in sin that grace may abound? By no means!"

A second false application is the popular claim: "See, I told you that righteousness is relative. All Lot needed to do to be called righteous was to be slightly less bad than the evil people around him." There is no biblical support for this view.

A third false application is the claim that the standard for righteousness changed in the New Testament. "Lot is never called 'righteous' in Genesis; he's only called righteous in the new era where grace covers every sin." That claim runs counter to the point of 2 Peter 2 and to the teaching of Jesus in Matthew 25.

What are the legitimate applications of Lot's story?

Grace means that no person need be defined by his worst acts and decisions. Just as David was forgiven of adultery, lies, and murder, Lot was forgiven by God. Just as Saul was forgiven for persecuting the church, we can be forgiven through grace (Rom 5:6–8). God remains better at forgiving than we are at sinning.

Even the most heinous and embarrassing of sins, from a human perspective, are not beyond the scope of God's grace. Lot's story helps us understand and appreciate 1 Corinthians 6:9–11. Lot helps us avoid the deadly error of declaring ourselves too evil for God to save.

Lot emphasizes a powerful lesson we first learn from Noah in Genesis 6. One person, one family, can choose righteousness even when the world around us rebels against God. We would never claim that this is easy, but we know that it is possible through God's grace (Titus 2:1–14).

Lot reminds us that there are limits to God's grace. One could make the case that Lot stayed in Sodom and became a civic leader because he thought he could make a godly difference (Gen 19:1). The men of Sodom did not see it that way: This fellow came to sojourn, and he has become the judge (Gen 19:9)! After being warned by the angels, Lot lingered—trying to save his sons-in-law, but he could not. Even Abraham could not save the evil cities. When the appointed Day of the Lord comes, whether ultimately or in some partial measure, the door of grace closes (Matt 25:1–13, 2 Cor 5:9–11, 2 Pet 3:1–13). God's kindness in warning us of the deadliness of sin, the brevity of life, and the certainty of judgment stands as a huge act of grace.

## Discussion Questions

1. Is it fair to Scripture to describe Lot's story as a story of grace? Has this lesson made the case?
2. Even though grace triumphed, why is it important to remember that Lot bore terrible consequences for his sins?
3. Why would God choose to describe Lot as righteous and godly in 2 Peter 2? Why share this information with us?
4. Why might some over-apply Lot's story to the subject of grace?
5. Why might some be tempted to discount Peter's teachings about the righteousness of Lot?

## Note

"The Darker Side of Sin." Pages 15–21 in *Visions of Grace: Stories from Scripture*. Florence, AL: Heritage Christian University Press, 2019.

# Service

# Chapter 17

## *A Contemplation on Faithful Quietness*

### co-authored with Laura S. Bagents

I f our minds are biblically tuned, we love faithful quietness. Every time we see it, we're impressed and intrigued. How did this happen? How did this person gain such depth of faith and spirit? Why do I still have so far to go? Do the quiet ones realize how their example shines in its uniqueness? Do they know how impressive and challenging they are to those of us who want to follow them? Could they teach us if we asked? If so, would they need words? To what degree would the learning process flow from observation and imitation? Are some born with a disposition toward faithful quietness, or can God teach that virtue to anyone who's willing?

Perhaps another question must precede the ones above: What do we mean by "faithful quietness"? In its ultimate form, it's described in Isaiah 53:7–8, which says of God's suffering servant,

He was oppressed, and he was afflicted, yet he opened
not his mouth: like a lamb that is led to the slaughter, and
like a sheep that before its shearers is silent, so he opened
not his mouth.

It was perfectly embodied by our Lord during His life
in the flesh (John 19:8–11, Luke 23:9, Mark 14:61 &
15:3–5, Matt 27:12–14).

Faithful quietness, as described in 1 Peter 2:18–25, is
faith-filled imitation of Christ's example, following "in his
steps." It includes

- putting "away all malice and all deceit, and
  hypocrisy and envy and all slander" (1 Pet
  2:1).
- consistently living as "a chosen race, a royal
  priesthood, a holy nation, a people for his own
  possession" (1 Pet 2:9 & 12).
- abstaining "from the passions of the flesh,
  which wage war against your soul" (1 Pet
  2:11).
- being "subject for the Lord's sake to every
  human institution" (1 Pet 2:13).
- putting "to silence the ignorance of foolish
  people" by living in keeping with God's truth
  and Christ's character (1 Pet 2:17 with
  2:11–12).

- graciously enduring wrong and choosing to do right, no matter what others do (1 Pet 2:18–21).
- foregoing both vengeance and demanding one's rights (1 Pet 2:22–25, Rom 12:19–21).
- utterly entrusting ourselves "to him who judges justly" (1 Pet 2:23).
- choosing incorruptible spiritual beauty and substance over appearance and posturing (1 Pet 3:1–6).
- deserving or not, treating everyone with respect and compassion (1 Pet 3:7–12).

For followers of Jesus, faithful quietness is summarized by Galatians 2:20:

I have been crucified with Christ. It is no longer I who live, but Christ who lives in me. And the life I now live in the flesh I live by faith in the Son of God, who loved me and gave himself for me.

Everything is by Him, for Him, through Him, under His authority, and to His glory. Everything we think, say, do, and desire flows from our love for Him and our trust that He is saving us.

# The Choice of Quietness

It would be hard to argue that Lamentations isn't the Bible's darkest book. The title itself offers a major clue. Yet within this painful book are amazing rays of heavenly light. Few shine as brightly as Lamentations 3:25–27.

> The Lord is good to those who wait for him, to the soul who seeks him. It is good that one should wait quietly for the salvation of the Lord. It is good for a man that he bear the yoke in his youth.

The faithful of Jeremiah's day did not choose the yoke of bondage that plagued them. They were victims of a corrupt system created and maintained by self-serving leaders and many evil followers who just went along. The faithful of Jeremiah's day had no way to stop God's righteous judgment on their nation. Even the prayers of Moses and Samuel could not change the outcome (Jer 15:1). Even the presence of Noah, Daniel, and Job could not stop the coming destruction (Ezek 14:14).

The faithful could not stop the invasions, the siege, the devastation, and the deportation, but God allowed them an amazing choice—the ability to choose how they would endure those inevitable horrible events. They could choose to "wait quietly for the salvation of the Lord." They could choose to "bear the yoke" in faith, learning its lessons and welcoming the ways God would use it to shape them. They could choose to see a degree of good in the end of the world as they knew it. In the face of the unthinkable—including the destruction of God's temple— they could choose faith and hope. Jeremiah 30:10–11a reads,

> Then fear not, O Jacob my servant, declares the Lord, nor be dismayed, O Israel; for behold, I will save you from far away, and your offspring from the land of their captivity. Jacob shall return and have quiet and ease, and none shall make him afraid. For I am with you to save you, declares the Lord.

The question was (and is) never, "Will the hard times come?" THE QUESTION was (and always will be), "In a world of loss and woe, will we hold on to the promises of God?" Will we shape our attitudes and conduct by our knowledge of God's power, love, and goodness? Will we choose to live in faithful quietness when those around us rage?

Are we overstating the level of choice that God affords us? Consider Psalm 131. Some Bibles offer the caption, "I have calmed and quieted my soul." 131:2 says in effect, "I won't overprocess. I'll reject worry. I won't pretend that somehow I can figure everything out so that it all makes sense." It expresses a commitment to let God be God because we will never be up to that task. Psalm 131:3 is brilliant: "But I have calmed and quieted my soul, like a weaned child with its mother, like a weaned child is my soul within me." The meaning is clear: "There's been a process, and it hasn't been pain-free. But I've moved to the next phase of life, to the next level of understanding. I will not get stuck in the choice to fight reality. I will move forward by adjusting to and embracing God's reality." At the spiritual level, that's the key to faithful quietness.

Many passages affirm the choice of faithful quietness. Ecclesiastes 4:6 does so inferentially and poetically: "Better is a handful of quietness than two hands full of toil and a striving after the wind." Isaiah 7:4 offers a direct command to King Ahaz as the kings of Israel and Syria were about to attack him: "Be careful, be quiet, do not fear, do not let your heart be faint because of these two smoldering stumps ..." Ahaz had far more choice of attitude and trust than most realize.

Isaiah contributes notably to our understanding of faithful quietness as a choice and a blessing. Decades before the die of God's judgment against Judah was cast, Isaiah faithfully proclaimed, "For thus says the Lord God the Holy One of Israel, 'In returning and rest you shall be saved; in quietness and in trust shall be your strength.'" Sadly, ancient Judah was unwilling to embrace this promise, but it was there to be embraced. God has never offered an empty promise. His ancient people put their trust in false prophets, corrupt leaders, military alliances, and the physical temple. And they found no calm, peace, quiet, or salvation. We love the powerful reminder of the steadfast connection between quietness and trust in God.

Isaiah speaks of a coming king who will reign in righteousness. Though there will be major resistance,

Then justice will dwell in the wilderness, and righteousness abide in the fruitful field. And the effect of
righteousness will be peace, and the result of righteousness, quietness and trust forever. My people will
abide in a peaceful habitation, in secure dwellings, and in
quiet resting places (Isa 32:15–18).

Ancient Judah may have heard these words primarily
in terms of a restoration of their nation after a period of
captivity; their longer meaning has always been spiritual.
There's biblical linkage between righteous, justice, peace,
and quietness. And what of trust per verse 17? It speaks of
trust in the coming king, the righteous king, the King of
Kings.

As we think of values and behaviors linked to quietness, we must not neglect Zephaniah 3. In a paragraph
extolling Israel's joy and restoration, the prophet writes,

Sing aloud, O daughter of Zion, shout, O Israel! Rejoice
and exult with all your heart, O daughter of Jerusalem!
For the Lord has taken away the judgment against you;
he has cleared away your enemies. The King of Israel,
the Lord, is in your midst; you shall never again fear evil.
On that day it shall be said in Jerusalem: Fear not O
Zion, let not your hands grow weak. The Lord your God
is in your midst, a mighty one who will save; he will
rejoice over you with gladness; he will quiet you by his
love; he will exult over you with loud singing (Zeph
3:14–17).

What joy! What hope! God will save, remove fear, and bring joy. But the sweetest line is "He will quiet you by his love." And that tremendous blessing even comes with a song of celebration!

## Why Would Anyone NOT Pursue Faithful Quietness?

Obvious answers abound. For those who do not believe in God, the question will never be addressed. For those who do not trust the truthfulness of Scripture, there can be no standard by which to evaluate the question or confidence in the biblical calls for this holy pursuit. The voice of the world is LOUD, persistent, and pervasive. Many have come to prefer the din of constant distraction. The pursuit of calm, peace, and focus must seem infinitely boring. Some may reject the pursuit of a quiet mind/spirit as unbiblical, as belonging to Eastern religions, whether Zen or otherwise. We would argue that such thinking unfairly conflates biblical meditation (Ps 1, Phil 4:8, 1 Tim 4:15) with one of its opposites.

Some have never been invited to pursue quietness. They lack a frame of reference from which to consider that option. They don't even know that option exists. For others, it remains stunningly difficult to think and live on a level more advanced than the world around us. For many Christians, the world—at least its better aspects—is the standard (Rom 12:1–2, Col 3:1–11). No doubt some have attempted the pursuit but found it too difficult. They lacked the wisdom, knowledge, foresight, or support system to continue the effort.

The first line of Lamentations 3:25 may offer a deeper reason that some forego pursuit of a quiet and gentle spirit. "The Lord is good to those who wait for him, to the soul who seeks him." Waiting for the Lord—an essential aspect of a quiet spirit—isn't just waiting; it also includes continual seeking of God's grace and God's truth. It is genuine work and commitment. It includes unwavering hope in God's goodness and salvation. To wait quietly on the Lord is hardly a passive stance toward life. There's massive spiritual activity surrounding the choices to "fear not" and "wait quietly for the salvation of the Lord." And that activity isn't just internal. It includes helping other believers embrace that peaceful perspective as well.

## New Testament Commands to Seek Faithful Quietness

On the level of principle, the Sermon on the Mount has much to contribute. It's no stretch to liken a quiet spirit with meekness (Matt 5:5). Both loving enemies and embracing an ethic of non-retaliation flow from a deeply God-centered heart (Matt 5:38–48). Matthew 6:1–18 subtly promotes the virtue of "quietness" as it warns—three times—against the temptation to seek public praise. As Matthew 6:25–34 argues against worry, it strongly advocates the advantages of a settled, quiet, and trusting heart. It's no leap to propose that those of a quiet and deep spirit are best prepared to forego both unbiblical judging and the ever-present danger of unfairly comparing ourselves to others (Matt 7:1–5).

Several passages more overtly prescribe quietness. "... Aspire to live quietly, and to mind your own affairs, and to work with your own hands, as we instructed you, so that you may walk properly before outsiders and be dependent on no one" (1 Thess 4:11–12). While certainly not a command to become silent and irrelevant (Matt 5:13–17), the passage warns against making oneself the center of attention as if the gospel depended on our personal charisma. Paul wanted the Thessalonian Christians—and us—to be people of depth and substance, to be people of good reputation and trustworthy character. This message is strongly confirmed by 2 Thessalonians 3:11–12.

1 Timothy 2:1–10 also guides our thinking. A key reason Paul urges

> supplications, prayers, intercessions, and thanksgiving be made for all people [particularly] for kings and all who are in high positions [so] that we may lead a quiet and peaceful life, godly and dignified in every way.

Such lives would strongly align with God's desire that "all people be saved and come to the knowledge of the truth." We are not denying the ancient truism, "The blood of the martyrs is the seed of the church." Rather we affirm that the gospel has equal saving power during times of calm and peace when it can be shared neighbor to neighbor. 1 Peter 4:13–17 speaks powerfully to this both-and nature of evangelism and the benefits of living in "good conscience" with "gentleness and respect."

In terms of direct affirmation, we are blessed to remember 1 Peter 3:1–6, the text from which this book takes its name. We pay extra attention when anything is described as "very precious" in God's sight. And that is exactly how the text describes "the imperishable beauty of a gentle and quiet spirit." It's the very spirit demonstrated by the Lord Himself (Matt 11:29).

## Biblical Examples of Quiet Service

In addition to Jesus, what other examples of a gentle and quiet spirit stand out in Scripture? We think of Rebekah, who was "very attractive in appearance" (Gen 24:16), but equally attractive in attitude and spirit. Her politeness and acts of service gained the attention of Abraham's servant and led to her place in the lineage of David and of Christ.

We think of Esther. Ultimately, her queenly service was anything but quiet, but God chooses to remind us of her pleasing disposition and her humble decision to heed her adopted father's counsel (Esth 2:8–11). Even as she exposed Haman's plot and saved God's people, she did so with amazing restraint and decorum (Esth 5–6). She played—and never over-played—her crucial role in God's plan. Much the same can be said of Mordecai. With the possible exception of his unwillingness to bow to Haman, he is consistently presented as unselfishly blessing, serving, and protecting.

We think of the unnamed widow of Zarephath who acted against sight and common sense to bless the prophet Elijah (1 Kgs 17). As she acted in faith during a time of stunningly severe famine, "The jar of flour was not spent, neither did the jar of oil become empty, according to the word of the Lord that he spoke through Elijah." Admittedly, this lady's life was not always quiet. She became quite direct when her son died, and God raised the boy. It's our best judgment that one purpose of this amazing story is to remind us that a quiet spirit often flows from a soul that has grown deep and bold.

We think of the unnamed servant-girl of 2 Kings 5:1–4. All she needed to exact revenge on her captors was to keep silent. Rather than withholding crucial information, she told her mistress of the prophet of God in Samaria and opened a door to healing.

From the New Testament, we think of Mary, mother of Jesus, and her cousin Elizabeth. We know Elizabeth only as wife of a priest, mother of the forerunner of Jesus, and encourager of Mary (Luke 1:39–45 and 57–60). We see Mary snatched from obscurity to a vital role in God's plan, and we stand amazed by her faith, humility, and willingness to serve. "Then Mary said, 'Behold I am the servant of the Lord; let it be to me according to your word'" (Luke 1:38). Mary's song of praise (Luke 2:46–55) stands as one of the most beautiful and dynamic prayers in all of Scripture. For centuries, scholars have called that prayer The Magnificat!

We think of Tabitha, aka Dorcas (Acts 9:36–42). The text describes her as "full of good works and acts of charity." We learn a bit later that she sewed profusely. Those she blessed were not content to leave her dead; neither was God. Peter was summoned, God acted, and her resurrection "became known throughout all Joppa, and many believed in the Lord."

We think of Lydia. Acts 16 presents her as a business-woman, a homeowner, and a person of means. As soon as she and her household were baptized, she insisted that Paul and his co-workers accept the hospitality of her house. Though that plan was delayed, her heart was in the right place. She showed a servant's heart.

In the broadest of terms, we think of Hebrews 11:32–40. In terms of notoriety and public influence, it's a mixed text. It mentions Gideon, Barak, Samson, Jephthah, David, and Samuel by name. It mentions the prophets as a group and Daniel without using his name (Heb 11:33). It mentions people who conquered kingdoms and "put foreign armies to flight." It includes "women [who] received back their dead by resurrection." But it also includes unnamed victims of mocking, flogging, chains, imprisonment, and other afflictions. It adds those who lost their lives to stoning and sword.

What do we find remarkable about Hebrews 11:32–40? The named and the unnamed, the survivors and those who died, those with major public impact and those who died in obscurity—none are overlooked by God. All are counted precious by God. All are equally described in the phrase "of whom the world was not worthy." One need not be famous to be beloved, honored, and appreciated by God. The faithful who manifest a gentle and quiet spirit stand as pillars in the kingdom. Their examples make us better because they so beautifully honor God.

As we contemplate both biblical and current examples of a quiet and faithful spirit—particularly the example of Jesus Himself—we feel the pull of grace and opportunity. We work to live up to the high calling of scripture. And we welcome the ever-increasing influence of deeply spiritual brethren who consistently show us God's better way. Because we must keep growing toward Jesus, we deepen our commitment to trust God above all, especially above ourselves.

## Note

"A Contemplation on Faithful Quietness." Pages 16–24 in *A Gentle and Quiet Spirit: Festschrift for Barbara Dillon.* Florence, AL: Heritage Christian University Press, 2023.

# Chapter 18

## *The Church as Salt and Light*
### Matthew 5:13-16

We love Jesus's dynamic description of His church. It's not, "You should be the salt of the earth" or "You have the power to be the light of the world." Rather, the Lord called us to be what He has made us.

We think of salt as flavoring, enriching, and taste-enhancing. Colossians 4:6 comes to mind: "Let your speech always be gracious, seasoned with salt, so that you may know how you ought to answer each person." Just as Jesus "went about doing good," so do His disciples (Acts 10:38). Our conduct and our character enhance our communities. Our presence and examples bring out the best in others. Like Barnabas and Dorcas of old, we impact those around us for good.

Were we to lose our flavor, our Christian impact, we would fall under the condemnation of Matthew 5:13—we would be good for nothing. Or perhaps, we'd be even worse. We could distract people from the gospel and give them excuse to live outside Christ. Just as Titus 2:10 calls on servants to live "so that in everything they may adorn the doctrine of God our Savior," we know the importance of consistently walking "in the light as he is in the light" (1 John 1:7).

Though it is not the point of emphasis in Matthew 5:13, we also think of salt's preserving powers. Salt works against decay and corruption. Spiritual salt works against sin and death. Just as ten righteous souls would have spared Sodom and Gomorrah (Gen 18:32), we are blessed to contemplate the favor that God shows to all because of the presence of His people. It's the principle clearly taught in Genesis 12:1–3.

Fairness demands that we remember that salt also burns at times. Think of getting sweat in your eyes or into a cut as you do outside work on a hot summer's day. In this sin-damaged world, some will regard any spiritual salt as an irritant. They will object to how the presence of salt makes them feel. While it's never our aim to be irritating, sometimes it's a compliment to be considered a bother. It can speak of our distinctiveness in Christ and our faithfulness to Him (1 Pet 4:4, John 3:19–21).

The devil loves debilitating extremes. He will assert that you can't be salt without being salty, without being overly stout, disagreeable, and painful to others. He will invite some to embrace this model and to ignore John 13:34–35, Ephesians 4:31–32, and Colossians 3:12–17.

He will claim that truth trumps grace, love, and kindness. Others, he will invite to purposefully avoid the redeeming qualities of salt lest they be perceived as negative or judgmental. With them, he will claim that grace, love, and kindness trump truth. How blessed we are to recognize and reject his lies!

We love Jesus's description of us as "the light of the world" (Matt 5:14). This sin-damaged world is plagued by darkness. We see countless examples of what Jesus described as "blind leaders of the blind" (Matt 15:14). Life continually affirms the truth of Jeremiah 10:23 and Proverbs 16:25. Without guidance from above, things don't go well for us.

There's a huge compliment in Matthew 5:14 when Jesus says, "You are the light of the world." Think of John 1:4–5, "In him was life, and the life was the light of men. The light shines in the darkness, and the darkness has not overcome it." Think of John 8:12, "I am the light of the world. Whoever follows me will not walk in darkness, but will have the light of life." As long as Jesus was in this world in the flesh, He was the light of the world (John 9:5). Now, He describes His followers, His church, with the very same language! "You are the light of the world."

Of course, this is a wonderful testimony of the humility of Jesus. It's also a tremendous statement of His expectation for the church. We are to shine like a city set on a hill. We are to give light to all who are in the house. We are to let our lights so shine that men will see our good works and glorify our Father in heaven.

The second fact about our role as light in this world from Mathew 5:13 is, "A city set on a hill cannot be hidden." Christianity was born in a challenging region during a challenging time. The church faced daunting persecution (Acts 8:14, Heb 10:32–34, Rev 2:9–10). Still, Jesus describes His church as "a city set on a hill." The church is, as it were, a lighthouse. It lives, honors, and offers the light of truth and righteousness. It calls people toward the gospel and toward heaven. To use the language of Philippians 2:15, we are "children of God without blemish in the midst of a crooked and twisted generation, among whom you shine as lights in the world." That was true in the days of Jesus and Paul. God means for it to be just as true today.

Jesus moves from describing the Christian light as a city on a hill to speaking of it as a lampstand within a home. Its purpose is to give "light to all in the house" (Matt 5:15). We give light as we teach and live God's truth. We give light as we love and forgive one another. We give light as we "reprove, rebuke, and exhort, with complete patience and teaching" (2 Tim 4:2). We give light as we "admonish the idle, encourage the fainthearted, help the weak, [and] be patient with them all" (1 Thess 5:14), We certainly give light as we speak "the truth in love" and "grow up in every way into him who is the head, into Christ ..." (Eph 4:15).

Matthew 5:16 is both intentional and encouraging. We embrace God's command to let our lights shine. Our good works are purposeful, designed to help others see and honor God. Of course, we reject excess and self-centeredness as condemned in Matthew 6:1, 5, and 16. While rejecting pride and self-promotion, we acknowledge the tremendous teaching and motivational power of good works. Even secular people are inclined to believe what they see. It's tremendously challenging to ignore a consistently good and giving life.

The encouraging part of Matthew 5:16 is so easy to grasp. As the church is what the church should be, salt and light in this world, people will see our service in the name of Christ and will give glory to God. We know that a word of caution is needed. Not all will see, and not all who see will choose to glorify God. Some are very skilled at rejecting the Father, but all will have the opportunity to see and give honor. And some will give God the level of honor that includes believing His word and obeying His gospel.

We stand amazed that God gives us the honor of living for Him. What a gift to be able to help others recognize and appreciate the Creator, the Ruler of the universe, the Sustainer of all that is good, right, and holy.

We think of light as it enables and enhances vision. We see more clearly in the light. Psalm 119:105 celebrates the truth that "Your word is a lamp to my feet and a light to my path." Given human frailty, stumbling is a fact of life, but stumbling is lessened by adequate light. Stumbling is also lessened by staying on the path. And stumbling need not be fatal because our God is always there to lift us up.

Admittedly, light can sometimes challenge us. A car can look so clean in the garage, but sunlight shows all the spots and streaks. Our lives can look quite good when compared to the culture around us, but when we examine ourselves in the true Light, what we learn can really scare us. What a joy to remember John 3:16–17, Romans 8, and Ephesians 2:1–10. God's light is the ultimate truth and purity. God's light is also stunningly loving. He seeks our best and our salvation. He knows better than we do the dangers and costs of sin (Eph 6:12, Isa 59:1–2). He wants us to learn the joys of living as His church, His children (1 John 3:1–2).

Living as salt and light opens tremendous doors of spiritual opportunity. It's a blessed life here, but the ultimate blessings are unspeakably greater. And those blessings are eternal. Forever. Everlasting. Infinite. Unfathomable.

## Discussion Questions

1. What aspect of salt impresses you the most as you think about the church and each Christian as "the salt of the earth"?

2. What can we do together and individually to enhance our effectiveness as "the light of the world"?

3. Why would any church or Christian be tempted to hide his/her light?

4.  How would a person go about hiding his/her light? What would this look like in practice?

## Note

"The Church as Salt and Light." Pages 33–40 in *The Ekklesia of Christ: Becoming the People of God.* Berean Study Series. Florence, AL: Heritage Christian University Press: 2015.

# Leadership

# Chapter 19

## *Renewing Respect for Leadership*

M any people love to hate their leaders. They love their leaders when they recognize the need for focus, vision, and empowerment. But they hate what they sometimes see in leaders: the abuse of power, the frustration of stagnation, and the death of dreams. Strong language? Yes, and deservedly so. As goes the leadership, so goes the group. And that is particularly true in highly social, "voluntary membership" organizations like the church.

Leaders have clay feet. Abraham lied and re-lied about his relationship with Sarah (Gen 12 & 20). Once, he even laughed at the promise of God (Gen 17:17). Moses had the episode of excuse-making, a period of failing to delegate, and an occasion of failing to give glory to God (Exod 4 & 18; Num 20). Saul fell into abject rebellion (1 Sam 13 & 15). David fell into adultery and murder (1 Sam 11). Solomon fell into idolatry (1 Kgs 11). And many of the kings who followed made these early leaders look good!

The pattern continues in the New Testament. Peter denied (Matt 26:69–75). Thomas doubted (John 20). Barnabas, the very "son of encouragement," once deserted his Gentile brethren (Gal 2). Key members of Paul's inner circle fell away (2 Tim 4:9–16). Who can forget Diotrephes "who likes to put himself first," who tried to take the role that rightly belonged to Christ (3 John 9, Col 1:18)? As foretold in Acts 20:28, even elders in the church fell prey to Satan.

We also know the frailty of human leaders from our own experience. We've seen men whom we thought to be spiritual giants dissolve into pettiness. We've seen men we held in high esteem forsake the truth of God. We've seen men and ladies who were pillars of the church desert their families and shipwreck their faith.

We live in a cultural climate of diminishing respect for leadership. Some see Watergate as the watershed event. Others point to the ethical relativism and moral improprieties of subsequent administrations. We have learned that major politicians don't write their own speeches, and we have come to wonder if they even mean the words that they read. It's as if people now expect political leaders to lie.

The climate of diminishing respect for leadership has been fed by our homes. Wedding vows are not honored. Many parents are like the Pharisees of Matthew 23:3, "For they preach, but do not practice." As children see hypocrisy within their own homes, they begin to wonder, "Can I trust anybody? Is there anybody who tells the truth and walks the walk?"

In such a climate, is it possible to renew respect for leadership? Is it even desirable to make the attempt? What does God have to say on this matter?

## How Bad Can It Be?

Nobody knows the depth of the problem like God does. He created man "in his own image," with unlimited capacity for good (Gen 1:26–27). How His heart must break when He sees people falling so far beneath His standard and His will! We see that pain in Isaiah 1:10, when God calls the leaders of His chosen nation "rulers of Sodom." With biting clarity, God condemned the leaders of Isaiah's day: "For those who guide this people have been leading them astray, and those who have been guided by them are swallowed up" (Isa 9:16). With equal clarity, God chastised His rebellious people for demanding that their religious leaders stop seeing and teaching accurately and rather, "Speak to us smooth things, prophesy illusions" (Isa 30:8–11). They were living a deadly cycle: bad leaders were creating bad followers, and bad followers were demanding bad leaders.

In light of these truths, Isaiah 3 is stunning! Because His people refused to demand, respect, and follow sound leadership, God promised to remove qualified leaders.

Even worse, God promised to remove their respect for leadership.

> I will make boys their princes, and infants shall rule over them. And the people will oppress one another, every one his fellow and every one his neighbor; the youth will be insolent toward the elder, and the despised toward the honorable (Isa 3:4–5).

And what would be the people's response to this void of leadership and respect for leaders? They would demand that someone step up to lead. At the same time, they would beg to be spared the mantle of leadership (Isa 3:6–7). Given the ongoing mistrust, microscopic scrutiny, and unrealistic expectations frequently faced by leaders, we understand their reluctance to serve.

Without respect for leadership, there can be no effective leaders. Without respect for leadership, God's people move toward destruction. At the same time, people commonly get the level of leadership that they deserve. Self-willed and rebellious followers beget self-willed and rebellious leaders. The cycle is vicious. And even in better circumstances, power often corrupts. Yet, despite all these pitfalls God has not given up on the concept of human leadership.

## The Biblical Basis for Leadership and Respect

Leadership goes back to the first page of Scripture. As God blessed Adam and Eve, He instructed them to "... fill the earth and subdue it, and have dominion over the fish of the sea and over the birds of the heavens and over every living thing that moves on the earth" (Gen 1:28). By creating male and female in two stages, God foreshadowed the husband's leadership in the home. Genesis 18:19 reminds us that Abraham's leadership was crucial to God's plan for him:

> For I have chosen him, that he may command his children and his household after him to keep the way of the Lord by doing righteousness and justice, so that the Lord may bring to Abraham what he has spoken to him.

Though God could have accomplished the exodus through any number of means, He called Moses as leader of the march to freedom. As Moses aged, Moses himself recognized the need for a succession of leadership. "Let the Lord, the God of the spirits of all flesh, set a man over the congregation ..." (Num 27:16). God concurred, telling Moses to lay his hand on Joshua, to inaugurate him before the people, and to "invest him with some of your authority ..." (Num 27:18–23). How wise of Moses to recognize the need to empower the next generation of leaders!

We know the terrible cycles of sin and pain that Israel

endured after the death of Joshua and his peers. To the best of our knowledge, there was no leadership succession plan. Judges 17:6 and 21:25 summarize the matter: "In those days there was no king in Israel. Everyone did what was right in his own eyes."

Jesus understood the ongoing need for leadership. Without the protection of a shepherd, the flock will be scattered and vulnerable (John 10). Who could forget Matthew 9:36, "But when he saw the crowds, he had compassion for them, because they were harassed and helpless, like sheep without a shepherd"? And quoting Zechariah 13:7, Matthew 26:31 adds, "Then Jesus said to them, you will all fall away because of me this night, for it is written, 'I will strike the shepherd, and the sheep of the flock will be scattered.'"

Jesus provided for leadership after His return to heaven. Ephesians 4:11–12 summarizes,

> And he gave the apostles, the prophets, the evangelists, the shepherds and teachers, to equip the saints for the work of ministry, for building up the body of Christ.

The early church followed Jesus's example. The complaint by the Hellenists against their Hebrew brethren was met by appointing another level of servant leaders in the church (Acts 6). Paul is legendary for his ongoing training of future leaders, even as he traveled the Empire preaching the gospel. One of his trainees, Titus, was left on Crete specifically "so that you might put what

204 Getting My Heart Right With God

remained into order, and appoint elders in every town as I directed you ..." (Titus 1:5). Leadership is near and dear to God's heart.

Respect for leadership is also dear to God's heart. Though no human leader is perfect, God commands respect for leaders. Even after Saul was rejected as king and the spirit of God left him, David rightly refused to raise his hand against the Lord's anointed (1 Sam 24:8–10 & 26:8–12). In fact, he executed the man who claimed credit for killing Saul (2 Sam 1).

The New Testament consistently commands respect for leaders, even for those who fail to honor God. Based on Exodus 22:28, Paul apologized for speaking harshly of the high priest Ananias, even though Ananias deserved condemnation for breaking God's law (Acts 23:5). Jesus instructed the people to do what the scribes and Pharisees told them to observe because "The scribes and the Pharisees sit on Moses's seat" (Matt 23:2). While Jesus condemned the hypocrisy of these leaders, He recognized the need to respect their position of leadership. Even though Paul had suffered unjustly at the hands of civil authority, Romans 13:1–2 commands respect for leadership.

> Let every person be subject to the governing authorities. For there is no authority except from God, and those that exist have been instituted by God. Therefore whoever resists the authorities resists what God has appointed, and those who resist will incur judgment.

Peter echoes those words in 1 Peter 2:11–17. Certainly, these passages do not demand blind, unthinking obedience to civil authority (Acts 4:19–20 & 5:29). However, the principle of respect for leadership stands firm. Respect for God demands respect for leadership.

## Renewing Respect for Leadership

Given the flaws of human leaders and the spirit of our age, how can we renew our respect for leadership? First, we can pray for our leaders. 1 Timothy 2:1–4 reads,

> First of all, then, I urge that supplications, prayers, intercessions, and thanksgivings be made for all people, for kings and all who are in high positions, that we may lead a peaceful and quiet life, godly and dignified in every way. This is good, and it is pleasing in the sight of God our Savior, who desires all people to be saved and to come to the knowledge of the truth.

No one is above, beneath, or beyond our prayers. Even if the leader for whom we are praying resists God's will and is totally unaffected by our prayers, we will be blessed for having prayed. Consistent, fervent prayer will shape our hearts in the image of Christ. Prayer will keep us from becoming bitter or feeling powerless. If prayer changes nothing else, it always changes the pray-er.

We can deepen our submission to our God. All respect flows from respect for God. If his faithfulness to God could help David show a measure of respect to the man who was unjustly seeking his life, we can respect the flawed leaders among us. If Paul could urge respect for the authorities who beat him, we can show respect for those who sometimes disappoint us.

We can work with godly leaders to accomplish godly goals. Leadership, like virtually everything, looks different from the inside. Sometimes we assume that leaders have more wisdom, power, stamina, and confidence than they actually possess. People have been known to say, "If I were in a position of leadership, then we'd never ____ or we'd always ____." "Never" and "always" are seldom good words when talking about the behavior of others. It's virtually impossible to make people do what we know they should do. Even leaders who have tremendous relational and legitimate power are not always followed. Good leaders, especially godly leaders, listen to those who work with them.

In a closely related vein, we can encourage our leaders. Sometimes we fall victim to the simplistic paradigm: "It's the job of leaders to encourage followers." Those words often carry a degree of accuracy. Leaders commonly offer more encouragement than they receive. However, there is no reason for the flow of encouragement to be one way. Even though Paul was a great leader, he longed to visit the Christians in Rome, "that is, that we may be mutually encouraged by each other's faith, both yours and mine" (Rom 1:12). Paul was encouraged by the devoted service of the household of Stephanas. When Stephanas,

Fortunatus, and Achaicus visited him, Paul says, "They refreshed my spirit as well as yours" (1 Cor 16:13–18). The care extended to Paul by the Philippians not only encouraged him, but it was also received as "a fragrant offering, a sacrifice acceptable and pleasing to God" (Phil 4:10–20). Colossians 4:7–15 lists numerous brethren who encouraged Paul during his imprisonment. The entire Thessalonian church encouraged Paul through their "work of faith and labor of love and steadfastness of hope in our Lord Jesus Christ ..." (1 Thess 1:3). That passage reminds us of 3 John 4, a verse that can be claimed by every faithful leader: "I have no greater joy than to hear that my children are walking in the truth."

Similarly, our leaders can encourage us by giving us every reason for respect. Leaders whose faith is worth following deserve imitation (1 Cor 11:1 & 16:15–16; Heb 13:7). Those who "set the believers an example in speech, in conduct, in love, in faith, in purity" foster ever increasing respect (1 Tim 4:12). Consider Ezra and Nehemiah. These men put their lives on the line for the work of God. They put their hands to task and worked as one of the people. They were open, ethical, and above reproach. They embodied the truth of Philippians 2:3–4. While even they had their critics, good people must have found them easy to follow, easy to love, and easy to respect. When their words come from God and their practice matches their words, leaders give us every reason to respect their leadership.

In renewing our respect for leadership, we can

remember that we, too, are flawed. To be blunt, if we were perfect, we might have the right to demand perfect leaders. Since we're not perfect, we better find a way to work with the leaders that we have. Hebrews 13:17 offers biblical guidance:

> Obey your leaders and submit to them, and be submissive, for they are keeping watch over your souls, as those who will have to give an account. Let them do this with joy and not with groaning, for that would be of no advantage to you.

Disrespecting and grieving our leaders is both unbiblical and unprofitable. Respecting godly leadership, on the other hand, is profitable. It's part of being in the will of God. It expresses trust in God. It calls for the best in others. And, it is the will of God; it prepares us for greater roles of leadership and service. The bottom line is clear. Respect for God demands respect for leadership. It always has and it always will.

## Discussion Questions

1. In your judgment, what has contributed most to the modern decline in respect for leadership?

2. Has the modern decline in respect for leadership been exaggerated? Understated? Explain.
3. To what degree should we trust our leaders? What factors should determine the level of our trust?
4. What can the church do to raise up better (more godly, more consistent, more effective) leaders?
5. Do brethren tend to have unrealistic expectations of their leaders? Explain.
6. Do Christian leaders tend to have unrealistic expectations of themselves?
7. It has been asserted that people often get the level of leadership that they deserve. Agree or disagree and give reasons for your answer.

## Note

"Renewing Respect for Leadership." Pages 75–82 in *Renewing Respect: Rediscovering a Forgotten Virtue.* Edited by Bill Bagents. Nashville: Gospel Advocate Company, 2009.

# Chapter 20

## *Leadership Flows from Followship*

The story is told of a brash young lieutenant who railed on his troops unmercifully. His abusive behavior was obvious to all. After far too many episodes, his colonel brought the lieutenant's attitude and actions to the attention of a wise old general. The general's comment was priceless: "It's no surprise that he's a poor lieutenant; he wasn't much of a private either."

Every good leader, save God Himself, is first a good follower. The Lord Jesus beautifully demonstrated this truth while He lived on the earth in the flesh. At age twelve He told his worried parents, "Why were you looking for me? Did you not know that I must be in My Father's house?" (Luke 2:49) Because it is God's will that children follow the lead of their parents, "... He went down with them and came to Nazareth, and was submissive to them ..." (Deut 5:16, Luke 2:51).

Jesus consistently lived the beautiful submission of

"followship." When the tempter came to Him, each attack was answered with a quote from Scripture (Matt 4:4, 7, 10). Man lives and is guided "by every word that comes from the mouth of God." "You shall not put the Lord your God to the test." "You shall worship the Lord your God, and him only you shall serve." Each of these quotations includes a direct statement of submission to the Father.

The gospel of John dramatically documents the "followship" of Jesus. John described the Lord as "... the only Son of the Father, full of grace and truth" (John 1:14). Jesus used similar words to foretell His own sacrificial death: "For God so loved the world that he gave His only Son ..." (John 3:16). Jesus told His disciples, "My food is to do the will of him who sent Me, and to accomplish his work" (John 4:34). Clearly, Jesus came to earth of His own free will. Philippians 2:5–11 reminds us that He "... emptied himself, taking the form of a servant, being born in the likeness of men." Yet, Jesus Himself gave God the Father all the honor for His coming. It is amazing how many times the Lord describes Himself as being sent by the Father (John 7:16 & 28, 8:16 & 42, 9:4).

Jesus claimed no authority apart from the Father. "Truly, truly, I say to you, the Son can do nothing of his own accord, but only what he sees the Father doing" (John 5:19). "My teaching is not mine, but his who sent me" (John 7:16). "... I do nothing on my own authority, but speak just as the Father taught me" (John 8:28). John 12:49–50 adds,

> For I have not spoken on my own authority; but the
> Father who sent me has himself given me a command-
> ment—what to say and what to speak. And I know that
> his commandment is eternal life. What I say, therefore, I
> say as the Father has told me.

Jesus lived in perfect obedience to the Father. "For I have come down from heaven, not to do my own will, but the will of him who sent me" (John 6:38). John 8:29 adds, "And he who sent me is with me. He has not left me alone, for I always do the things that are pleasing to him" (John 8:29). Though the Father gave Him full power over His own life, "lay it down" and "to take it up again," even in the face of the cross, He willingly submitted to the Father's will (John 10:17–18, Luke 22:42).

The power of "followship" is evident throughout Scripture. Joseph's service and submission paved the way for his advancement in the house of Potiphar, in the Egyptian prison, and in the service of Pharaoh. Joshua's faithful service to Moses prepared him to be the next leader of God's people. Can we ever know how much Elisha learned or how much his faith grew during his years as Elijah's servant? The Lord Himself chose twelve, not only as witnesses to His life and teachings but also as leaders-in-training.

Paul continued the Lord's pattern in his mission to the Gentiles. From John Mark to Timothy, Titus, and count-less others, he worked to develop leaders by letting young men serve with him. While Paul did not invent the practice of mentoring, he used the concept powerfully.

The concept of "followship" found broad expression both in Paul's life and in his teaching. We remember 1 Corinthians 11:1, "Be imitators of me, as I am of Christ." 1 Corinthians 16:15–16 continues the theme. Because those of the household of Stephanas "devoted themselves to the service of the saints," the believers in Corinth were instructed to "be subject to such as these, and to every fellow worker and laborer." In urging Timothy to "set the believers an example," Paul strongly implies that the believers ought to follow Timothy's excellent example (1 Tim 4:12). Philippians 3:17 is even more direct: "Brothers, join in imitating me, and keep your eyes on those who walk according to the example you have in us."

What implications should we draw from these truths? Strong leadership flows from strong "followship." Until we learn the cost and the value of humility, submission, obedience, and loyalty, we are not ready to lead. Until we willingly follow those whom we should be following, we have no right to lead.

Strong leadership develops over time. There is no instant version. Godly character cannot be molded overnight. The thick skin and soft heart of a godly leader are forged in the fires of experience and time.

"Followship" is, itself, a powerful form of leadership. We could call it self-leadership. Good "followship" demonstrates that we have a strong measure of self-control, a strong measure of selflessness. We can also say that good "followship" encourages good leadership.    It brings out the best in our leaders. It urges them to keep learning and growing. It empowers them to lead more effectively. More than that, good "followship" sets an example that urges others to follow God.

Every good leader is first a good follower. That eternal truth flows from God Himself. Jesus lived it, and so do His disciples.

## Note

"Good Leaders Are Good Followers." *Gospel Advocate* 146/8 (August 2004); 12–13.

# Chapter 21

## *A Plea for Grace and Fairness as Older Generations Assess Younger*

## An Introduction

From a secular perspective, stout expressions of disappointment in younger people by older generations date back more than 2,500 years. The following is attributed to Socrates (470-399 BC), the founder of Western philosophy:

> Children, they have bad manners, contempt for authority; they show disrespect for elders and love chatter in place of exercise. They no longer rise when elders enter the room, they contradict their parents and tyrannize their teachers. Children are now tyrants.[1]

Though commonly beloved as summarizing the ancients' view of the young, linkage to Socrates has been deemed false. Still, many have deemed it too important—

realistic and helpful—to be dismissed. The concept seems to be, "If Socrates didn't say it, he should have. It conveys truth." While that approach is utterly unscholarly, it says much about the human tendency to love purportedly ancient quotations—whether specious or real—that support what we prefer to believe. We need to be better than that.

More reliably, in *Art of Rhetoric* Aristotle wrote,

> They [young people] are high-minded since they have not yet been humbled by life, nor have they experienced the force of necessity ... they think they know everything, and confidently affirm it ...[2]

A Google search quickly offers hundreds of similar statements.

Worklife. Amanda Ruggeri, "People have always whinged about young adults. Here's proof." https://www.bbc.com/worklife/article/20171003-proof-that-people-have-always-complained-about-young-adults Accessed 9.3.22 10:15 AM.

Joe Gillard, "The 2,500-Year-Old History of Adults Blaming the Younger Generation." https://historyhustle.com/2500-years-of-people-complaining-about-the-younger-generation/ Accessed 9.3.22 10:30 AM.

Ruggeri includes a list of somewhat contradictory "reasons" for the ongoing and pervasive criticism. Older generations have asserted that younger people are lazy, think they know best, are too cautious, are too confident, have elevated expectations, complain too much, spend too much, and want to live in adolescence forever. She offers the list as reporting the historical record, without asserting its fairness or accuracy. She's purposefully painting with a very broad brush.

The Ruggeri post is best read in concert with Katie Bishop's 2022 article, "Are Millennials and Gen Z Weaker than Boomers and Gen X?" https://www.bbc.com/work-life/article/20220218-are-younger-generations-truly-weaker-than-older-ones Accessed 9.3.22 10:00 AM.

Bishop wisely cautions older generations to reflect on the possibility that their standards of evaluation may be outdated—reflecting, at least to some degree, a world that no longer exists.

## Biblical Underpinnings

We cannot rightly deny the danger of generational apostasy. Joshua 24:31 and Judges 2:7 are virtually identical: "And the people served the Lord all the days of Joshua, and all the days of the elders who outlived Joshua ..." Judges 2:10 is tragic:

> And all that generation were gathered to their fathers. And there arose another generation after them who did not know the Lord or the work that he had done for Israel.

Indeed, that's the infamous Judges Cycle—the people

sinned and were oppressed, they cried to God for deliverance, and God delivered them through a judge, but they eventually forgot the Lord and fell back into sin. Generation after generation repeated the terrible pattern. The devil would love for us to forget that terrible tendency so that we might perpetuate it. Few errors are as foundational and effective as the denial that danger is even possible.

Students of the Bible may find the assertion of a 2,500-year history of older generations questioning the wisdom of "newbies" amusing. Consider 1 Kings 12. As Rehoboam rejected the measured advice of the elders in favor of the stout threats recommended by the young men, he divided the kingdom. He lost 10 of the 12 tribes. Surely this documents that "Wisdom is with the aged, and understanding in length of days" (Job 12:12).

But the matter isn't that simple. 1 Kings 12 resonates powerfully with the next chapter. In 1 Kings 13, the advice of an old prophet leads to the disobedience and death of a young prophet. Read together, the message is not "always trust the older leaders because they are wiser." Rather, the point is "trust the word and wisdom of God rather than men—whether young or old—always."

Jeremiah indicates awareness that his prophetic service was likely to be limited by his young age. "Ah, Lord God! Behold I do not know how to speak, for I am only a youth" (Jer 1:6). God rejected his reasoning as out of hand (Jer 1:7–8).

Though much more recent, 1 Timothy 4:12 documents the temptation for older Christians to look down on younger disciples, especially those filling a teaching role. "Let no one despise your youth" is followed by excellent practical advice: "But set the believers an example in speech, in conduct, in love, in faith, in purity." Like every young Christian, Timothy needed to show his mettle. And older Christians need to appreciate and respect such stellar examples.

Though stunningly complimentary of twelve-year-old Jesus, Luke 2:47 speaks to the tendency to underestimate young servants of God. Among the teachers in the temple, "All who heard him were amazed at his understanding and his answers." His grasp of God's word and His duty to know and serve God (Luke 2:49) were amazing.

## Explanations: Why Do Older Generations Often Disparage Younger Ones?

There's wisdom in the list offered by Ruggeri above. Young adults can lack the seriousness, work ethic, and task-orientation of their elders. Ironically, they can be both over-confident and overly cautious—either alternatingly or at the same time. There can be strong pull to see oneself as functionally invincible, hyper-skilled, globally aware, and able to solve virtually any problem. This tendency can present as arrogance, and arrogance always invites mistrust and opposition.

Many older adults fear change. At the least, it's unfamiliar. Some could come to view all change as negative and dangerous. Younger generations often welcome change and work to foster it. Those who embrace or expedite change can be seen as enemies of those who are threatened by it. "Change for the sake of change" can seem—and feel—unwise, unnecessary, and unbiblical. If that feeling is strong and personalized, any effort toward change—even positive and godly change—can be viewed as an attack on truth.

From a biblical perspective, changes in methods and applications can be errantly lumped with rebellious departure from God's "ancient paths." "Thus says the Lord, 'Stand by the roads, and look, and ask for the ancient paths, where the good way is; and walk in it, and find rest for your souls'" (Jer 6:16). We have seen this verse misapplied to reject the use of PowerPoint and Prezi in Bible class, reading scripture from a device rather than a printed Bible with a black leather cover, teaching the gospel via social media, and preachers choosing to dress more casually.

Sociologically and psychologically, members of an older generation can feel that we are being unwisely or prematurely replaced by younger disciples and leaders. In light of Hebrews 9:27, 2 Corinthians 4:16–5:8, and 2 Timothy 4:6–8, there's a healthy dose of reality in such feelings. Unless the Lord comes, death and "the passing of the torch" are inevitable. But the inevitable need not be negative or depressing. How we love the Bible's mentoring stories—Moses and Joshua, Elijah and Elisha, Jesus and the twelve; Paul and Timothy, Titus, etc. We see the same principle for ladies in Titus 2:3–5. We love to see congre-

gations where spiritual formation and leadership development are blessed, biblical, and intentional.

It's also possible for members of an older generation to
lament our inevitable physical and mental decline.
Younger people can—wrongly—assume that physical challenges always include diminished judgment. Especially
when these happen in concert, older Christians can feel
unfairly judged and unwanted. When we feel unfairly
treated, we commonly question the motives, character,
and agenda(s) of those behind that treatment. And negativity begets negativity.

Without blanket endorsement, we value the following
words from cultural anthropologist Margaret Mead: "Also
characteristic of the modern world are the acceptance of
generation breaks and the expectation that each new
generation will experience a technologically different
world." (47) And, "Innovations in technology and in the
form of institutions inevitably bring about alterations in
cultural character." (48) Her conclusion:

> Even very recently, the elders could say: "You know, I
> have been young and *you* have never been old." But
> today's young people can reply: "You have never been
> young in the world I am young in, and you never will be
> ..." (49)[3]

Both for better and for worse, the rate of societal
change continues to escalate. The young often understand
nuances of their culture in ways that escape those of us

who are older. Social nuances can be amazingly subtle and can turn on a dime. If we lack sufficient frame of reference, they will be invisible to us.

Culturally speaking, even within the church, the environment we grew up in seems normal to us. From hairstyles to clothing to communion ware to hymnals to comfort level with technology—including preferred means of communication, each generation differs. To a degree, each successive generation defines itself through such differentiation. These preferences and traditions are often ascriptural—the Bible does not speak to them. We must honor every tradition given to us by God (2 Thess 2:15 and 3:6), but we must never defend a human tradition as if it were mandated by God (Matt 15:1–9, Titus 2:8–10). We must be willing to discern and respect the difference.

## Dangers: How Could Generational Disparagement Harm God's Church?

If older Christians adopt a blanket us-versus-them approach to younger Christians, morale is damaged, and unity is threatened. John 17 and Ephesians 4:1–6 will not be honored. The body of Christ will suffer.

The devil owns the title "accuser of our brothers" (Rev 12:10). He needs no help in that role. While we "reprove, rebuke, and exhort," we do so biblically "with complete patience and teaching" (2 Tim 4:2). Our approach is always "speaking the truth in love" (Eph 4:15), even as we "abide in the teaching of Christ" (2 John 9) and "contend for the faith that was once for all delivered to the saints" (Jude 3).

Generational mistrust impedes mentoring. It creates opportunities for the devil to steal souls from Jesus. It supports fundamental unfairness. Remember Genesis 6; the entire world—that entire set of generations—was wholly wicked, except for Noah and his family. Consider the faithful remnant in the days of Isaiah and Jeremiah. Think of Ezekiel 18:20,

> The soul who sins shall die. The son shall not suffer for the iniquity of the father, nor the father suffer for the iniquity of the son. The righteousness of the righteous shall be upon himself, and the wickedness of the wicked shall be upon himself.

No family and no generation is monolithic and homogenous.

Generational mistrust destroys both the synergy and the example of generational respect. Within any family or congregation, the oldest, "the middles," and the youngest have respective strengths. They have varying talents and perspectives that contribute to faithful service, fellowship, and evangelism. God knew what He was doing when He "arranged the members in the body, each one of them as he chose" (1 Cor 12:18). Unloving competition and division are the way of the world. God's church must be different! Titus 2:1–10 commands the older generations within the church to help—particularly to educate—the younger.

## Recommendations: How Can We Minimize Harm and Maximize Generational Synergy?

We can resist the temptation of blanket criticism. The young are not wrong or inferior in every action and assertion—few individuals and no generation are that consistent (Job 32:1–37, esp. 32:6–14; Luke 2: 40–47). We dare not let even major flaws blind us to major strengths and blessings. We can consistently notice, support, and celebrate every younger Christian who stands firmly in Christ (Phil 2:19–30).

We can address the danger of assuming that we already know what "those young folks" will say to us (Prov 18:13). Satan can tempt us to think that we've heard it all before. He'll even quote parts of Scripture: "What has been is what will be, and what has been done is what will be done, and there is nothing new under the sun ..." (Eccl 1:9).

We can remember that change can be biblical and God-honoring (Acts 11:19–21, 2 Cor 5:17, 2 Pet 1:5–11). By definition, repentance is change of mind and heart accompanied by the corresponding change in behavior. Every improvement in surgical technique or physical therapy is a positive change. So is every strengthened relationship and step toward Jesus (1 Thess 4:9–10, 2 Pet 1:5–11).

We can rejoice that God helps people grow in wondrous ways; with God's help, people can become wiser and more spiritual. Think of the young John Mark who left the mission team versus the more mature young man who had become "very useful to me for ministry" (Acts 13:13, 15:36–41; 2 Tim 4:11). It's great that he grew, great that Paul noticed his growth, and great that the Spirit had Paul record this rich set of examples for us.

We can choose to employ the tremendous power of our words with wisdom, consistency, and intentionality. Given the wisdom of age and our knowledge of God, we can be instruments of grace for younger generations (Eph 4:29–32, Col 4:6). We can model the superb virtues of weighing our words and thinking before we speak (Prov 15:1, 29:11 & 20; Jas 1:19).

We can also remind everyone—especially ourselves—that sometimes the less we say, the better (Prov 10:19, 17:27–28). What an important example for us to set in this shrill and uncivil world! At times silence can be cowardice and sin, but at other times it's absolutely golden (Ezek 33:1–11, Acts 20:27, Eccl 3:7).

We can enthusiastically embrace the biblical mandate to help grow the next generation of believers (Deut 6:7, 2 Tim 2:2, Titus 2:1–9). They need us, we need them, and God is honored when both parties lean into that opportunity. When we were young, so many of us were mentored, forgiven, tolerated, pulled upward, prayed for, and stubbornly loved by the generations who came before us. We have boatloads of blessings to pay forward.

As he assesses generational challenges in the church—particularly in ministry—the devil perversely enjoys the downward spiral of "divide and conquer." He loves false assumptions, impugned motives, and an atmosphere of constant mistrust. Oppositely, the Lord commands, blesses, and loves the upward path of spiritual service and synergy (Eph 4:11–16). He knows we're better together because He made us that way.

## Endnotes

[1]  https://quoteinvestigator.com/2010/05/01/misbehave/ Accessed 9.4.22 2:50 PM.

[2] Aristotle. *Art of Rhetoric. II.12.11.*

Aristotle. *Art of Rhetoric.* Trans John H. Freese. 23 vols. LCL. Cambridge: Harvard University Press, 1926–2020.

[3] Mead, Margaret. *Culture and Commitment: A Study of the Generation Gap.* Garden City, NJ: Natural History Press, 1970.

# Chapter 22

*Inviting Respect as Younger Generations Interact with Older*

## An Introduction

For thousands of years, older generations have criticized those who follow them.

1 Worklife. Amanda Ruggeri, "People have always whinged about young adults. Here's proof."
https://www.bbc.com/worklife/article/20171003-proof-that-people-have-always-complained-about-young-adults Accessed 9.3.22 10:15 AM.

Joe Gillard, "The 2,500-Year-Old History of Adults Blaming the Younger Generation."
https://historyhustle.com/2500-years-of-people-complaining-about-the-younger-generation/ Accessed 9.3.22 10:30 AM

For just as long, younger generations have hated that. No one loves being described as lazy, wasteful, entitled, arrogant, disruptive, disrespectful, irresponsible, or unappreciative—and the list could be far longer. Even if many within a given generation manifested such qualities, an impressive and encouraging number would not. Negative "clumping and lumping" is stunningly unfair. Every generation includes people of cultural, spiritual, and intellectual excellence.

This chapter is true to its title. It invites younger generations to show skill, respect, wisdom, and awareness as they interact with those they view as old. Admittedly, that calls for a second mile, sacrificial approach. But the Bible offers strong support for choosing that God-honoring and Christlike path (Matt 20:26–28 & 22:36–40, Phil 2:3–4, 1 Pet 5:5–7). Plus, the worldly alternatives never work. They each include the seeds of their own destruction.

## The Power of Contextualizing

Contextualizing—seeing the big picture, trying to walk a bit in their shoes, working to understand their perspective—can help younger Christians offer more patience toward and communicate more effectively with older saints. It can make challenging people and situations feel less bizarre and hopeless. There's often major blessing in remembering some common assumptions of older generations. Please note that we're painting with a very broad brush here.

Older generations can view even biblical change as rejecting their values and depreciating their contributions.

They can see change as purposefully and prematurely pushing them toward obsolescence. They can personalize even highly effective new ministry applications as intentionally making their lives more challenging. For many who are older, change is far from a positive and comforting concept. And younger generations tend to love change.

There's a strong tendency to see the practices and traditions with which we grew up as normal—the way things should be. To the degree that's true, "newness" is unfamiliar, frightening, and abnormal to older generations. There's also a tendency to think that changes in methods and applications are attempts to undermine or ignore biblical mandates. We remember the "show your work" mandate from our math classes. The principle fits here; show older brethren how anything new in ministry fits with and flows from Scripture. If the biblical connections aren't there, don't pretend or stretch. Stay on the solid ground of biblical authority.

From the perspective of the young, there's also a strong tendency to personalize opposition and resistance. That can manifest as "These old folks are not just opposing progress, they're opposing us!" On a spiritual level, it translates into "They're opposing God." This double—or is it triple?—wham can be potent.

A fascinating aspect of contextualization is future-focused. As younger Christians work to love, bless, and coexist with older Christians, they're wise to remember that, unless they die young or the Lord returns, they will one day be part of an older generation. In terms of sowing and reaping (Gal 6:6–10), how do you want to be treated then? In terms of Luke 6:37–38,

> Judge not, and you will not be judged; condemn not, and you will not be condemned; forgive, and you will be forgiven; give, and it will be given to you. Good measure, pressed down, shaken together, running over, will be put into your lap. For with the measure you use it will be measured back to you.

Talk about an opportunity! God offers reciprocity on steroids bathed in grace. Conversely, what a warning! Play petty, hate, and harm, and expect way worse than you've sown. On the most basic practical level, how we treat older generations teaches younger generations how to treat us.

## How Can Younger Christians (Servants and Leaders) Build Bridges to Effective Intergenerational Ministry?

Create authentic opportunities to express appreciation to older generations (Rom 13:7). Even God loves honoring the honorable. Biblical examples abound. "Enoch walked with God, and he was not, for God took him" (Gen 5:24). Everyone else in Genesis 5 has a death reported, but not Enoch. "But Noah found favor in the eyes of the Lord" (Gen 6:8). In a world engulfed in evil, one good man stood out. "Have you considered my servant Job, that there is none like him on the earth, a blameless and upright man, who fears God and turns away from evil?" (Job 1:8) "Abraham believed God, and it was counted to him as righteousness—and he was called a friend of God" (Jas 2:23).

Jesus followed the Father's excellent example. "He marveled and said to those who followed him, 'Truly I tell you, with no one in Israel have I found such faith" (Matt 8:10). "Take heart, daughter; your faith has made you well" (Matt 9:22). Remember the outstanding praise of Peter in Matthew 16:13–19 and of the church in Smyrna (Rev 2:8–11).

Not that the Bible needs external support, but both common sense and the social sciences support the power of legitimate praise to build relationships and strengthen love. Applied generationally, mindset becomes so important. If we commit to seeing the good in others and praising that good, we train our minds to look for the best in others. As a bonus, it trains others to look for the best in us. In large measure, we see what we choose to see.

Offer strong biblical support for needed changes (1 Pet 4:11). If a program or activity doesn't flow from the authority of Christ, it's not a path to spiritual blessing (Col 3:17). We respect the fact that biblical principles are just as authoritative as precise direct commands. We appreciate the fact that God can authorize specifically or generically (Matt 18:18–20; Gal 6:10; Phil 2:1–4; Titus 2:14, 3:8 & 14). We never play fast and loose with Scripture. And we never want to forbid what God allows (Rom 14). Our goal is to do His will His way.

Some congregations have sacred cows—preferred and time-honored practices that are ascriptural, that is Scripture says nothing about them. Examples include certain items of furniture, styles of communion ware, styles of sermons or song leading, processes and procedures for selecting elders or preachers, who can or can't drive the church van, who can or can't have a key to the church building or the church office, even choices of Bible translations.

If a practice is truly ascriptural, we can live with it whether we love it or not. The big issue isn't living with it; rather it's how we choose to live with it. We highly recommend love, grace, and patience. Good humor is welcome as long as it never approaches ridicule or sarcasm. Hills of judgment and preference are never worth dying on (Rom 14, Phil 2:3–4). They're not even worth stressing over. I've lived long enough to enjoy—very quietly—the death of several sacred cows. I've been blessed to see excellent people—young and old—endure "the non-ideal"—still speaking of ascriptural matters—for the sake of peace and unity. God has, does, and will bless their good hearts. With full respect to both 2 John 9 and Jude 3, we should not attend every argument or battle to which we're invited (2 Tim 3:22–26, Titus 3:9–11). And when a stand must be taken, we take it in love, humility, and trust in God (1 Thess 5:14, 2 Thess 3:14–15, Jude 9).

Be a person of sound character (1 Tim 4:11–16). Bluntly, be someone worth listening to because of your faith, service, wisdom, and humility. Be someone who is hard to ignore because you live 1 Peter 4:11; you consistently teach—and live—"as one who speaks the oracles of God." Be known as a peacemaker (Matt 5:9), an encourager (Heb 10:24), a truth-teller (2 Tim 4:2, 1 Pet 4:11), and a truth-doer (Ps 15:2, 2 Cor 13:8, 1 John 1:6).

Be an avid listener. James 1:19 is golden: "Know this, my beloved brothers: let every person be quick to hear, slow to speak, slow to anger ..." Nothing connects people more quickly or more deeply than heartfelt listening. Listening is love (1 Cor 13:4–11). Listening shows respect. Listening shouts, "YOU MATTER. I VALUE YOU." This is particularly true when younger servants of God listen to older servants. We old people assume that we have something to offer, and we want to share it with you. We want you to want to hear it. We need for you to hear it.

Admittedly, we sometimes say too much. Listen anyway. We sometimes repeat and re-repeat. Listen anyway. It's an investment that pays huge dividends. Occasionally, you will learn something important. Even if you don't, you'll create a relational environment where your voice becomes more powerful. Most good folks are highly reciprocal—if you listen to me, I'm obligated to hear you. The better you listen, the more you model good values and the more you obligate me to hear you well. It's major win-win synergy.

Be gracious, flexible, and willing to yield with the sphere of human judgment. Present all ministry ideas with humility. Welcome input. Listen powerfully, especially when we don't like what we're hearing.

Likewise you who are younger, be subject to the elders. Clothe yourselves, all of you, with humility toward one another, for God opposes the proud but gives grace to the humble (1 Pet 5:5).

If we can't submit to one another, we have not truly submitted to God.

Always practice gracious communication in every aspect, especially toward older Christians (1 Tim 5:1–2 & 19, Heb 13:17). There's a story my father loves to tell. A local farmhand had advanced in years; so had Dad. As the worker was slowly going about his chores, Dad said, "Old folks' time [meaning pace] is different." The man didn't miss a beat in replying, "Old folks' EVERYTHING is different." I've now lived long enough to know that's true. Wise young ministers appreciate those differences. They repeat and reinforce as needed. They explain and field questions as many times as needed. They patiently validate without frustration or manipulation. When frustration comes—sorry, but it will—they take it to prayer and seek God's relief.

"Better to ask forgiveness than permission" can be both a danger and a temptation. In its extreme, it allows bullying and bulldozing. Neither of those fits a household and a body headed by Jesus. The principles of Ecclesiastes 3:1–11 fit beautifully here. Seek God's wisdom and God's pace. Bringing people with us as we grow toward Jesus is the path of patience, kindness, gentleness, and love. It's also the path of respect, unity, and peace. It builds up without tearing up.

Speaking of pace, we're wise to appreciate the fact that the pace of change is a major generational factor. Younger generations tend to be physically, psychologically, and socially nimbler than the older. The zeal of youth can shout, "Get 'er done yesterday!" with insufficient attention to planning and prayer. It's rare to hear the younger say, "We can't do that because we've never done it before." The younger mindset is more often, "Let's try it BECAUSE we've never done it that way before." Older generations may need more undergirding and soak time than younger. Bottom line: Be patient. It's often true that good things come to those who wait.

God's sense of time is not ours, and God is always on time. Whether it's a change in ministry role or a change in a mission program, outreach activity, or addition to (or subtraction from) an eldership, one of Satan's classic ploys is to feed the "I'm ready, we're ready, the path is clear, what's everybody waiting on?" mindset. A common version is, "I've earned my degree—or two. I've been in this role for three years. I know I'm ready for a bigger challenge. Why hasn't God opened that door for me yet?"

While I can't claim to know the mind of God, several thoughts present themselves. We humans have a terrible tendency to overestimate ourselves (Jer 17:9, Rom 12:3). We have a wicked tendency to think that bigger is always better. The issue is never the size of the congregation we serve; it's always the faithfulness with which we serve where we are. We never know when God is protecting us from ourselves. The lady I married isn't the first one I dated, but she's the best one for me. I've had "career adjustments" that looked and felt terrible in the moment but proved to open amazing doors. Romans 8:28 is richer and more substantial than we'll ever know.

Learn that "no" sometimes means "not yet." The following is classic from church lore. A young minister presents a great idea in an elders' meeting, and it barely gets noticed. Six months later, one of the elders presents the same idea and it's lauded as wonderful. Sadly, that usually gets told as a pain story—"I was ignored and disrespected." Gladly, there's opportunity to reframe and find a major victory. The prayer of appreciation goes something like this: "Thank you, Lord, for letting me play a small role in this victory. I'm not sure if I was planting, watering, or both six months ago (1 Cor 3:6), but it's such a blessing to be on Your team. Please help me to see and support this victory to Your glory. Please help me remember that it was never about me." For a pleasant double-down, after the prayer, call a trusted friend and share the victory with him or her. God is the best validator in the universe. He has wondrous ways of setting things for the good of the kingdom. We're so extra-blessed to remember that in times of challenge.

## Conclusion

Given the prevalence and persistence of generational challenges, we're under no illusion that we can make them disappear—even within the church. Happily, we have no doubt that God can always help us be better than this sin-damaged world. We're blessed to employ biblical practices and principles to minimize unhealthy generational conflict. We're also blessed to remember that all conflict isn't bad. Sometimes it's a path to identifying growth points and building trust.

Every effort at godliness is profitable, even if results are slow or not yet visible (1 Tim 4:8, 6:6). God always blesses godly effort. He can use every process of spiritual growth and expression of love to grow us. And we never know when faithful effort will blossom into impressive victory.

# Scripture Index

# Acknowledgments

When Dr. Ed Gallagher inquired about the interest of Heritage Christian University Press in publishing a select compilation of his articles and essays, our response was both immediate and positive. His idea sparked an unintended consequence; I was asked if I might like to follow his example. I appreciate both the idea and the invitation.

Along with Laura Bagents, my wife and frequent co-author, the staff of Heritage Christian University Press greatly blessed the process.

Appreciation is expressed to Gospel Advocate and 21st Century Christian for their permission to include updated versions of Bible class lessons that they had published previously.

# Also by Bill Bagents

*Always Near: Listening for Lessons from God*

by Bill Bagents

*Revisiting Life's Oases: Soul-Soothing Stories*

by Bill Bagents

*Welcoming God's Word: Reading with Head and Heart*

by Bill Bagents

*WHAM! Facing Life's Heavy Hits: Thirteen Old Testament Encounters*

By Bill and Laura S. Bagents

*WHAM! Facing Life's Heavy Hits: Thirteen New Testament Encounters*

By Bill and Laura S. Bagents

*Equipping the Saints: A Practical Study of Ephesians 4:11–16*

by Bill Bagents and Cory Collins

*Counseling for Church Leaders: A Practical Guide*

by Bill Bagents and Rosemary Snodgrass

*Easing Life's Hurts* 2nd ed.

by Jack Wilhelm and Bill Bagents

CYPRESS

To see full catalog of Heritage Christian University Press
and its imprint Cypress Publications, visit
www.hcu.edu/publications